South America Mi Hija

Also by Sharon Doubiago

POETRY

Hymn to the Cosmic Clothesline, 1978
Visions of a Daughter of Albion, 1980
Hard Country, 1982
Oedipus Drowned, 1988
Psyche Drives the Coast, Poems 1975-1987, 1990

STORIES

The Book of Seeing with One's Own Eyes, 1988
El Niño, 1989

South America Mi Hija

SHARON DOUBIAGO

University of Pittsburgh Press

Pittsburgh • London

The publication of this book is supported by grants from the National Endowment for the Arts in Washington, D.C., a Federal agency, and the Pennsylvania Council on the Arts.

Published by the University of Pittsburgh Press, Pittsburgh, Pa. 15260
Copyright © 1992, Sharon Doubiago
All rights reserved
Manufactured in the United States of America
Second printing, 1992

Library of Congress Cataloging-in-Publication Data

Doubiago, Sharon.
    South America mi hija / Sharon Doubiago.
       p.   cm.—(Pitt poetry series)
    Includes bibliographical references.
    ISBN 0-8229-3671-2 (cloth).—ISBN 0-8229-5450-8 (pb)
    1. South America—Description and travel—Poetry. I. Title.
II. Series.
PS3554.O814S68   1991
811'.54—dc20   90-20875
                                                    CIP

A CIP catalogue record for this book is available from the British Library. Eurospan, London

Excerpts from *The Heights of Macchu Picchu* by Pablo Neruda. Copyright © 1966 by Jonathan Cape, Ltd. Reprinted by permission of Farrar, Straus and Giroux, Inc. and Carmen Balcells Agencia Literaria.

The author and publisher wish to express their grateful acknowledgment to the following publications in which some of these poems first appeared: *ACM (Another Chicago Magazine)* ("Pluto and Demeter"); *Bombay Gin* ("Peru"); *Bumbershoot Literary Magazine* ("Mamacocha"); *Calapooya* ("Everybody Lost Heart, Anxiously Waiting for Death"); *Calyx* ("In a Land Where Virgins Are Named Mama," "The Laughless Rock," "My Queen of Hades"); *City Lights Review* ("Amazon," "Compadrazgo Means Spiritual Link Between Two People," "The Shining Path"); *Compages* ("Maybe Love Was Present Only Among the Poor and Women," "The Task of Poetry Is to Overcome Government"); *Electrum* ("Descent: La Violencia"); *Mid-American Review* ("The Bridge of San Luis Rey"); *The New Settler Interview* ("Hija"); *Quarry West* ("Love Poem to Strong Wind, Amerrique," "Nuestro Ché: The Monroe Doctrine," "They Drive with Their Horns").

"Huaca" originally appeared in *Cradle and All: Women Writers on Pregnancy and Birth* (Boston: Faber and Faber, 1989).

"Descent: La Violencia" was reprinted in *Open Places* (Columbia, Mo., 1986). "Love Poem to Strong Wind, Amerrique" was reprinted in *Women at the River* (Tegucigalpa, Honduras: Editores Unidos, 1990).

Book design by Jane Tenenbaum.

for mi hija, Shawn Colleen Doubiago
for mi hijo, Daniel Clarke Doubiago

para todos los niños

Love that is not political is not love.
—Don Pedro Casaldaliga, bishop of São Felix, Mato Grosso, Brazil

Sube conmigo, amor americano
—Pablo Neruda, *The Heights of Macchu Picchu*

Alberigo Vespucci, because he associated the Indies with gold, changed his name upon retirement to Amerigo Vespucci. "Amerrique" is an indigenous name that means "strong wind," and that is the source of the genesis myth as recounted in the Popul Vuh.... The people living on the east coast of what is today Nicaragua were the Amerrique people living at the foot of the mountains that created the wind that inspired the myth that today gives everyone of this hemisphere an identity that in turn affects language and perceptions.
—Zoë Anglesey, "Central to America"

In 1979, declared the International Year of the Child by the United Nations, approximately 122 million children were born. Within twelve months, one of every ten of these infants was dead—a victim of disease, starvation, poverty and other preventable diseases.
—*Parade Magazine*

Contempt is the weapon of the weak and a defense against one's own despised and unwanted feelings. And the fountainhead of all contempt, all discrimination, is the more or less conscious, uncontrolled, and secret exercise of power over the child by the adult, which is tolerated by society (except in the case of murder or serious bodily harm). What adults do to their child's spirit is entirely their own affair. For the child is regarded as the parents' property, in the same way as the citizens of a totalitarian state are the property of its government. Until we become sensitized to the small child's suffering, this wielding of power by adults will continue to be a normal aspect of the human condition, for no one pays attention to or takes seriously what is regarded as trivial, since the victims are "only children." But in twenty years' time these children will be adults who will have to pay it all back to their own children. They may then fight vigorously against cruelty "in the world"—and yet they will carry within themselves an experience of cruelty to which they have no access and which remains hidden behind their idealized pictures of a happy childhood.
—Alice Miller, *Prisoners of Childhood*

I could not love in each being a tree
with its small fall on its shoulders (the death
*   of thousands of leaves),*
all the false deaths and resurrections
without earth, without abyss:
I wanted to swim in the widest of lives
in the freest of river mouths
and when little by little man denied me
closing his paths and doors so I could not touch
his wounded inexistence with my divining fingers
I came by other ways, street by street, river by river,
city by city. . . .
        —Pablo Neruda, *The Heights of Macchu Picchu* (author's
        adaptation)

The female void cannot be cured by a conjunction with the male,
but rather by an internal conjunction, by an integration of its own
parts, by a remembering or a putting back together of the mother-
daughter body.
        —Nor Hall, *The Moon and the Virgin*

I begin to sing of rich-haired Demeter, awful goddess—of her and
her trim-ankled daughter
        —*Homeric Hymn to Demeter* (seventh century, B.C.)

Yo hatch katchkani
Manan yo hatch katchkani
Chaimita tapukui

Contents

South America Mi Hija

I. The Road to Quito

In the earliest story
Persephone was playing with her companions and her mother
in a beautiful spring meadow
gathering lilies and violets
filling her basket and apron

when the earth gaped
and a great man appeared.

He raped her. Then carried her down
into his abyss.

Without a doubt the legend of El Dorado is the most beautiful, the strangest, and the most decisive in our history. Looking for that imaginary land, Gonzalo Jiménez de Quesado conquered half of what is today Colombia.
—Gabriel García Márquez

Of the time I spent in Bogotá I remember mainly images, indelible but difficult to connect.
—Joan Didion

You will be stopped and searched many times on the road to Quito.
—Mary Correal

1. Descent: La Violencia

Out the window, Colombia, out the window
the road beneath the window, the mountain village.
Out the window men on white donkeys, women in a crooked door.
Inside the window, back of the bus
I carry our daughter down the Cordilleras, the Andes.
Out the window armed farmers
carry marijuana to market.

Out the window Bogotá, city of thieves.
Out the window, the guns, the revolutionaries,
the lust of the police. Inside the window
the civil war, *you must take turns,* it is whispered,
*to sleep. Everyone has had someone
killed.*

Out the window the bus descends the continent.
Inside the bus the driver pilots an airplane.
We fly faster than last night's news warning of travel, we fly
over deep green valleys, mist-filled.
He sees around blind curves, he takes us over
flowering rock walls, landslides, a five-year-old boy
building an adobe brick house.
We fly past women washing clothes on a rock, we fly
above the clouds, above the road, how many days and nights
washed-out to Quito, around and around
the Cordillera Centro, how many nights
over the fog, over the coffee plants, over the jungle, the swollen rivers,
the cows and clouds streaming down the mountain side, the dark sky
of the East, over the grass huts perched on the abyss, over
these people who never traverse
to the outside. *If we go slow,*
it is explained,
the bandits will stop us.

Inside I dream I carry your daughter down the world.
Outside the girl Cartagena holds the Spanish explorers
at the continent's northern door
five days after they kill her people.
When they overcome her
every man rapes her
first. Inside our bodies
four hundred years of America.

Out the window a young man is boarding for Popayán.
Inside he falls in love with mi hija Shawn.
He begs us to stop in Ibagué where he lives.
When we say no he falls in love
with the black girl in front of him,
does not get off at Ibagué or Popayán, rides all night
with her to Tulcán.

Out the window Jesus bleeds
real blood and cries
diamond tears
down his naked body.
Out the window is a path
to the highest mountain
made by the crutches and canes of the crippled
who when they reached him
skipped away.

Out the window with each mile the state appears
beneath our tires, the police on the white road.
Inside the bus her uniformed hands
search briskly, professionally
not to admit the flesh, her hands on my breasts,
inside my vagina, I stare into her eyes,
her gunned hip
as she touches my daughter, the quick search
up the thighs. Beyond her
in the aisle, her brothers

search the men.
Outside as inside another woman weeps
for theft, I watch the long white road to Quito.

Out the window, Ibagué, city of music.
Out the window, poinsettia, avocado, banana, bougainvillea.
Out the window terraced mountains, eucalyptus, Easter lily, photo of Ché.
Out the window giant mimosa, smell of wood smoke,
a king dipped in gold, TURBAY Y SOMOZA, LA MISMA CASA!
Out the window clouds, the Spanish violin pouring
through the Western Cordillera.
Out the window the stimulants,
coffee, chocolate, sugar, marijuana.

Inside the red-fringed curtains
she sleeps on my shoulder
having gotten me from you.
Inside the shoulder the heart beats
to your rock n roll fiddle
that cries and wails
down the long continents
in a song I can almost hear
over the curve of earth.

In the front window the driver glows,
a mushroom in his white ruana,
spits to his violin, *gringas!* Inside
you drive me madly around curves, sawing
your instrument, my heart. Inside our daughter dreams
her future, her school, her men, her car.

Inside all night the boy from Popayán
touches through the seat crack
the breasts of the black girl from Tulcán
who travels with her ancient grandma
who gives us queso y pan that we eat

though the driver has warned
take food from no one. *Nada!*
You will be drugged. Then
you will be robbed. Inside
this body I yearn for your hands
on my breasts

as we descend west, south, down
the Western Cordillera, the road washed-out to Equador.
Inside the window of my heart
is a letter I write to you. Out the window
the Aquarius moon rises,
the constellation of your face,
my sprinting twin, mi amor norteamericano,
my Orpheus, you follow us down
the Andean night.

2. Someone waiting for me among the violins

I am with you in the small house of our life.
Musicians, your band of junkies,
one who has already died,
come to play.
But the music is gone from you.
The one who will die next
injects your violin
into his body.

Pregnant, I sweep the floor.
Holy music.
I sweep above you, the three of you,
then under you. Trinity.
Your lady of the broom.
Then through the community
that has come to hear you.

Slowly your violin materializes,
returns to you.
Joyful, with faith, we wait
to see what you will play.
Behind and above I look down
onto your bow
as it searches for the song.
The Earth spins,
sweeping the frail dancers off.
In your beautiful male body of patience,
truth's filament, you wait.
When the music comes, it comes
the great journey from Jupiter and the spheres,
it is more wonderful
than we dreamed.

But I forget myself. In the middle
of your ecstatic song, my sweeping dance,

my broomstick tangles with your bow
and the tragedy of our love,
that I am a mother
that you flee children and love
crescendos, and I find myself
outside our home
with your instrument.

I look down the ancient violin,
the two halves of the hemisphere.
The top begins to melt.
The bottom darkens, erupts
into flames.

3. Demeter and Persephone

In the morning waterfalls and her giggles
falling thousands of feet,
gorges so deep, mud slides,
sunrise, my maiden's shouts
down the greenest, the highest
Andes, silver

fall of the holy river
Guaitara
into and out of
clouds
churning the sun beneath us
music
ringing like a Spanish Piaf
and the brightest, most spectacular
rainbow. She squeals, the boy laughs,
"el arco iris!" the ends of

"the rainbow eye
of God," pour
violet, blue, green, yellow, orange, red
into the pots, godspots, holy *huacas* of two hills, arc
seven huts and people inside
who do not know
the colors that illuminate them.

                            "What
is the Third World?" she asked me
waking to daylight, Impiales, city
of three volcanoes, the headlines
STREET FIGHTING IN CARACAS! Revolutions
all around us, inching
toward Equador, down
the Inca Pipeline
dozens of busses, people

jammed on the tops, hanging off
the bumpers, amazing, waking
to this mass of humanity
beneath the United States

                         I didn't know
you were here

"Our blacks," Mary said in Bogotá
"live mostly on the coasts,
but we do not have prejudice
as you have it

against colors."

4. *Love, love, do not come near the border*

We are the only ones to cross to Equador.

"You must walk across the border"

a natural bridge over the Carchi River
Rumichaca
Royal Bridge of the Incas

Out the window we descend
a long morning to the frontera,
a desolate, colorless canyon,
"the driest, dustiest part
of the Andes," our things heavy,
the light, though early, a glare,
hard and hot.

Armed uniformed men
watch us come.
They lean against their border guard hut,
stroke their guns.
Comment.

Inside the hut naked girls, color of the canyon,
Playboy, Penthouse, Hustler,
are tacked with money
from the nations of the world
to every inch of wall.
The men take our pictures.
Then one tries to take me
to the other hut.
Suddenly, the girls stare down, twist torsos, open
vulvas, open mouths, cry

Mother! Sister!

"*Mi hija!*" I snap, grabbing her.
"*Mi hija!*"

They study our pasaportes.

"*Su madre?*"
They shrug their shoulders. "*Si,
su madre,*" sign our pasaportes,
chagrined

let us leave

5. Equal

Outside the borders guarded by pornography
Inside the borders guarded by the Goddesses

In Tulcán we walk the dreary morning streets
for coffee, my head pounding.
"The Panama Strip is still too rugged," he says
"to forge the Pan American highway. It took us
two months to walk it," and

                             Oh, then is born in me
the desire to walk it with her, mi Persephone

to know America, its core, mi Kore,
to walk the bridge, mi Isthmus of Darien
between the North and the South
to walk the borders
guarded by young girls.

Buseta now through thousands of Indians,
undulating sea of Panama hats,
this home of the U.S. fashion,
descending forever a dry river canyon
of grass roof huts on stilts,
villages of blacks, as if this were Africa, bundles and pots
balanced on heads, straight backs, washing clothes
down in the river naked, *Africa from Aphrodite!*
your naked babies playing in the Mira
on its way to the sea.

    I didn't know you were here

Now rain clouds gather and spread.
We climb back up the high passes,
Atuntaqui, Cotacachi, children staring off,
geysers blowing off, cows in the way, eucalyptus,
white roses, pink hibiscus, blue sky, geranium. Now the clouds

13

drop a little rain
in the small cobblestone street, spill
babies from every white adobe red tiled house. Should
I have a third child? Why
is it called
the Third World?

In the buseta's rearview mirror
I am the blond center
of dark travelers, even
mi hija is a brooding foreigner, my breakaway
daughter, the road now lined
with white crosses, those who did not reach
their destinations.

In the mirror of where we have been
I look like my mother. The old woman behind me
with a baby at her breast
makes me cry, this road like the road
to my childhood home, where I was most
unhappy, Escondido to Ramona
in hidden avocado, blooming crepe myrtle,
jacaranda, coconut palm, and all my life
that bird calling, is it
quail? No. Squawk, then a call:
nightingale.

Inside the window of my heart I remember
when I decided to trust you,
to overcome my despair
that men are unable to love
in the universal culture of sexism,
deeper, more ingrained than racism.

You loved me you said for teaching you this.
Only in the revolution of our love lives, you said,
is it possible to play the true music, to love

the earth.
You said the hatred of women
is the hatred of nature,
the fear of death.
You said this is the tragedy of Orpheus
who went all the way to Hell for his Love
but who in bringing her back to the world
in greed and lust, looked back. Objectified
her. Lost her. You said
Oedipus' love of his mother
was right instinct, his self-blinding
capitulation to the State,
to the Father, the despot
who kills the Son.

Out the window the earth spins.
Twelve hundred miles per hour. The exact
Middle, *Mitad del Mundo,*
Equador, equator. Equal
light
day and night. As above
so below. Yin and yang, male
and female.

Earth spins the balanced faces of the Otavalo
the gold chains around and around
the women's throats, sucks ash
from the volcano. "The quietest
Indian market in Equador. Bargaining
is done in hushed tones."
Even the babies
wear Panama hats, the reign of colors,
"Every cloth means something,"
and the men's long black braid,
six inches of shiny curl at the end
swishing their high butts, blue
ruanas, the shocking white pants, calf-high.

"They're rich, they have accounts with Macy's in New York City,
they drive Mercedes Benz." A beggar suddenly
at my window
drools on my arm, a face so crusted with dirt, scabs,
I can't find his eyes.
When I drop the coin in his hand
the driver curses me, gives a bill. Out the window

Otavalo, the enormous bundle
on the back of an old woman
bent double to the road, this burden,
myself, my daughter, my United States, you, my love
I carry down the continent.

But now as we pass
I look back to her, a face
looking up from the path
as pretty, as young
as Shawn Colleen, mi hija

shadow of clouds we race around

and around blind corners, a man
on a white horse galloping down
the steep road

to Cayambe, right over
the equator, hump
of the earth.

II. Quito

Persephone screamed for her mother.
When in her first fright she dropped the corner of her apron
and the flowers fell,
childlike, she felt the loss of them
as an addition to her grief.

The man was Pluto,
King of the Dead.
Persephone was made his Queen.

We have a little sister
and she hath no breasts:

What shall we do for our sister
in the day she shall be
spoken for?
—Song of Solomon 8:8

Beyond the equator everything is permitted.
—Fifteenth-Century Portuguese Proverb

1. The Wandering Virgin of Quito

a. Culture Shock

Out the window
two miles high
in a ring of volcanoes, *Pichincha,*
where the Equadorians defeated the Spanish, 1822

Out the window
the Virgin of Quito, *Cerro Panecillo*
the Wandering Virgin of Quito
in the September that is Spring
in the December that is Summer

Out the window, the market! A sudden halt!
Awake! In a sea of dark people, the blinding
equator light.
5:00 P.M.

Descend with your daughter
into men
who run in every direction, barefoot,
beneath Panama hats

to babies who wear Panama hats
tied to the backs of women
who wear Panama hats

through the June that is Winter

running   shouting   screaming   selling
in every direction
something important
the March that is Fall
(*Something important I wanted to say to you* . . .
the buseta already loaded and gone
back to their border

19

guarded by naked girls   our things
a pile in the urine   Now begins

the hissing

zz!   zzzzzzz!

spitting   drooling   crawling   pissing,   the men
(*Something important I must say to you, Shawn . . .*
up against any standing thing, the women
squatting, private
in the poncho

Now the smells
as we start with our map, our baggage
toward El Plaza de la Independencia, zz-zzzzzzz!
"the most beautiful plaza in South America"
a park bench to sit on, to gather
our wits

zz!   zzz!   zzzzzzzz!

men running at us   glaring   pointing
hissing, as we walk, heavy loaded,
up the steep narrow streets
their bright cloth shelters,
their faces, hidden beneath their hats,
at our waists, their fires in the cobblestones
at our feet   cooking

your dinner in this filth
your dinner in your rivers
of urine and shit
in this screaming crying fucking starving
all your life

la niña, su madre
like giant electric light bulbs

artificially illuminating
the natural world
the Wandering Virgin of Quito
her wild yellow hair flinging sparks
off the goddess shoulders
mi El Dorado glimpsed
through my own
blond wave

and the men
flying to our feet
in their ponchos
from the side streets
zz!   zzzzzzz!
zz!   zzzzzzz!

and the dark hatted men
reaching out to touch us
from their shops

zz!   zzzzzzz!

clutching erections, jumping
before us, zz! zzzzzzz!
unrelenting   unnerving   insulting
zz!   zzzzzzz!

"Try not to step in their piss," Demeter jokes
"Electrocution, zz-zzzzzzz!"

                Shar   on! Shar   on!

devastation and exhaustion
small miracles, the Hebrew
written on my throat
is read by wandering Jews.
We talk.
I am restored.

We reach the Plaza de la Independencia
I am the Rose of Sharon
and the lily
of the valleys

Now under our bench, *everlasting rose, our home*
zz!   zzz!   zz-zzzzzzz!
maniac eyes from the opposite bench
the collective rose
in the bushes that surround us
edifice of all mankind
crawling under   crawling over
running from the Cathedral
from every part of town

to gape   to hiss   to ejaculate
to discuss, *wandering virgins!*

our parts

zz-zzzzzzz!

b. Año Internacional del Niño

Inside the Cathedral of Santa Iglesia
"famous for its paintings,"
The Inquisition

execution by decapitation
of two children

At the boy's feet
his head is already lying
on a paper which flutters
the alphabet.

The girl is alive, not yet
beheaded, though her hands
are tied, though she is witness
to her brother.
Her magnificent countenance of resignation:
Saint.

The shirtless executioner lifts the sword.
At her feet the Word flutters.
In the congenial air of debate
men have gathered around this point:
*"Without the shedding of blood
there is no remission of sin"*
while the heads of a half dozen angels
wait.

c. Inside

> *Caylla llapi
> Pununqui
> Chaupi Tuta
> Hamusac.*

> In this place
> Thou shalt sleep
> Midnight
> I will come.

In the heart of old city, on Avenida Espejo,
Hotel Quitumbe.
In the doorway, a man asleep.
Or dead.
The price twice what the book lists
under Starvation Budget, twice
once again, our budget.
$3.75.

Lock the door, shower, the water's
cold. Clear the plugged drain. You've
picked up spit!
Find the dictionary, interpret the sign, ALWAYS
LOCK YOUR DOOR!
Count the money inside
your panty belts.

Beneath your window on Avenida Espejo
the boy barks
selling his wares, never
stops, hurts your ears, your tired
gringa minds
the high barbaric cry
of the insane.
Inside
on the bed
cry
      Mother
            Daughter

        though even now
        I don't take her in my arms
        I am the foolish mother

who brought her here, failed
my Little Innocent, my Fifteen Years.
Inside she dreamed
boys, islands, suntan, bikinis.
She dreamed sports cars, dinners by candlelight, boys
with money. Oh, she dreamed
Europe for which she worked
all summer, every check
into the bank.
All I did was sell our things
to come here.

I wanted her to know
the Third World. I wanted us
to know America, my last shot
as Mom. Europe and men, I said,
dinners, cars and wine
can wait.
Now out the window
the Third World
screams, it drools,
it pisses, it hisses, it
stinks.

"We're too poor," I admit at last
as everyone warned, to travel
this way. "Honey, we can leave.
We still have enough
to fly out of here.
Acapulco. Belize.
We'll have fun.   sun.   palms.
sea.   a real
vacation. We'll have
fantastic tans
when we get home."

"Let's think," she sobs,
"Twenty-four hours. Let's
sleep."

Out the window all night
the high screams of the insane boy
makes me think
I'll lose my
mind

Inside my blood loosens
the unborn flow
to the outside

inside she dreams me
how long how far
must I go
to know   *She wants*

me

2. I Am the Rose of Sharon

As the lily among thorns so is my love among the daughters.

a. I Opened to My Beloved

By night on my bed I seek him
whom my soul loveth.
I seek him
but I find him not.

I will rise now
and go about the city.
In the streets and in the byways
I will seek him.

I seek him
but I find him not.

The watchmen who go about the city
find me, to whom I say
Have you seen the One
I love?

A little after I pass from them
I find him
whom my soul loveth.
I hold him and will not let him go
until I have brought him
into my mother's house
and into the chamber of her
who conceived me.

I sleep, but my heart awaketh.
It is the voice of my beloved who knocketh, saying
Open to me, my sister, my love,
my dove, my undefiled. For my head
is filled with dew and my locks
with the drops of night.

I open to my beloved.
My soul faileth when he speaks.

My beloved withdraws himself
and is gone.

I seek him
but I cannot find him.
I call him
but he gives no answer.

The watchmen that go about the city
find me, they smite me, they wound me.
The keeper of the walls
take my veils from me.

I charge you, O daughters
if you find my beloved
tell him
I am sick with love.

b. Natural Shock

Wake to the earth
in boiling water
Earthquake!

Second story
the ceiling cracks, the many
repairs

Doze off again, wake
to another quake
This one stronger

Ten minutes
Another

Earth turning over, my daughter
beside me
Should I wake her?
How many stories, how many people
how much time
over us?

Somewhere
the record spinning
la norteamericana
Baez

diamonds and rust

We are moving into a wooden house.
My son and daughter are ten and seven.
I work on my grandmother's quilt, lay
her art, her diary, her Rose, her life
over them.

Now warm beneath it.
Brother. Sister.
Side by side.
He tells me something important.
She waits.
But before she is able to speak

the earth quakes and my Love loses
my grandmother's quilt.

3. Demeter

But mine own vineyard I have not kept.

a. Kidnapped

The dark people are floating on the rivers of urine
down an avenue named Mirror on the equator.
Beneath our window all night the high barbaric screams
of the boy insane

Niña, your back to me in this bed
You are so closed, so unknown
even to yourself
Mi hija, lost soul
of the world

I must talk to you.
I've brought you to the ends of Earth
to find the words.
I've given up everything, our home, our things
my man

You've given up everything
your home, your things, high school,
first boy

We've come this far
without money, language, or knowledge
How desperate we are
to come to this bed
beneath the world

How desperate you are
to pull me from him (how desperate I am
for his bed

to pull the words
from me

How desperate we are
underside of Earth, underside of love,
underside of self,
for the words

Our only guide: a lost little girl,
her high barbaric cries
pulling us down the world

b. Vac

I wait as I've always waited
as I awaited the eternity of your birth
for the words to rise
out of my rising flesh

I can hear the words
babbling in the creek of my womb
calling through vaginal space

But already you have tasted his pomegranate.
Long ago I ate the apple.
Fruit of the dumb, fruit of muteness, fruit of
Understanding: paralysed throat, O Girl
soul of all lost selves,
male and female

O Vagina
where the Goddess is lost

c. Omphalos

I can't see you
though you prance
imperious Amazon
here, so near the source

mammoth river, Earth's
largest river

When you speak to me
your voice
is a stranger's
to a stranger

you, daughter, so far from yourself
you, daughter, so far from me
you, daughter, so far from the world
in every human being

How could you not know yourself?
You were born, body and spirit, as One.
I know this. I witnessed
the Beginning.

Now I know again
that deepest, loneliest hole in the universe: *Daughter*

I was held in
when my need
sucked you here

d. Eleusis Dream of the Dance

You and all my daughters and nieces are here for the dance,
wild scented lilacs, violets, lilies, yellow irises,
brightest paradisiacal flowers
in this army quonset hut.
But I leave you, I need to get back
to my crazy, my shambly
bed.

Naked I lie down
beside my Love. Roses, crocuses, hyacinths.
All down his naked left side
my right side
our warm human flesh, the River.
I stare into the universe,
the northern sky of least constellations, least events,
the future, see my father
falling through them.

Then the shock, the panicked drowning:
The lover beside me is my brother!
Coming up for air I try to let go,
don't be afraid, it's okay, this is
good, the world
dies for our boundaries.
Brother. Sister. Mother. Daughter.
The world needs
our love.

But the door opens.
An old man enters
trips over our piled things,
crawls over the clutter of our lives,
lies down on the bed
at the right of our feet.
Dies.

A large male hand
strokes the right side of my mouth,
my small face in the crib,
hand so large
I suffocate.

e. At the Well of the Virgin

I wake back to this meditation, daughter,
your body of light, body of myself
lying there as in a haze of flowers.

The words are flowers
rooted in my throat, the flowers
you spilt when he raped you,
but when I open
there's only air, gasps, suck
of our sorrow, death of our Earth,
Sweetheart, you slip away
a lost language

through the hole of all eternity.
I see our two faces,
the One we've never found
the goddess *Mute,*
deepest, most familiar, most unknown, most betrayed

Mama

f. The Laughless Rock

In the earliest story
Isis was condemned to pregnancy,
to give birth in no time, no place

You wait for me to speak
My throat turns to stone

I want to say what all mothers
want to say to their daughters.
What all mothers must say
to their daughters

but are unable.
Why can't we speak?

Why do mothers betray their daughters
and thus themselves
all of life
the earth and all of time
the past and the future?

I am making the same betrayal
as my mother made of me
even now, though I have come this far with you
though you have come this far with me
though we have come this far together

though I have been thinking on this moment all your life
though you have waited all your life
though we know our necessary evolution

though you are raped, kidnapped,
though I hear you screaming

In you the secret turns to seed
In me, to stone.

g. My Queen of Hades

Hija, release of my ovary,
where are you now? Sleeping there
lightstruck, flamepillowed, maiden descended.
Outside on the balcony men serenade you.

Your soul loses me, wanders the night.
O wandering Virgin of Quito,
O city of ancient American stone,
northernmost outpost of the Inca soul.
I can hear her
whispering in the soil.

Are you dreaming my words?
If we continue south, if we fall
farther beneath the world
like the men who come here in search of gold,
will we find the words?
Are the words on the road?
Carried on the backs of llamas?
Will they erupt from the volcanoes
when we pass by?

My soul turns to stone.

Will the stones speak?

4. Dawn

I will always be on the equator
with my daughter.
I will always be with her
in Quito, Equador

the Otavalos gambling
in a circle around her

in Ejido Park beneath eucalyptus
squatted
to take her picture

and swarming
the jóvenes, the beggars, the starved, the sons

to look at
mi hija, her image
forever now on the equator

extraordinaire!
on a street named
Mirror

   Cocteau's mirror
   was the door to Hell in *Orpheus.*
   You said *mi hija*
   is *ma fia*

   the gang of men around the earth

   The Black Hand
   of vengeance blackmail

   that holds the daughters
   captive

cry and pray
mother-broke-asunder-by-the-quakes!
will we ever
get home?
will I ever return

to my love

        your home now, Madre
        this belt around Earth
        this hell
        the seasons

III. The Road to Lima

Persephone's screams were heard only by her mother
who then sought her daughter all the world over.
Brighthaired Aurora, when she came forth in the morning
and Hesperus when he led out the stars in the evening
found her still busy in the search

which was unavailing.

1. Pan American

a. They Drive with Their Horns

The earth spins
at its middle the Valley of Volcanoes,
spins the balanced faces of the Otavalos.
Inside my daughter giggles, lots of young men.
The moon rising in the Fish
plucks from inside my heart a music, washes
with its cosmic light the incredible Equador
thousands and thousands
in white knee pants, blue ponchos, Panama hats
streaming down the lunar land, twelve thousand feet the Andes
the local bus descending
to Perú.

The driver and I are the only ones awake.
Descending and descending all night the freezing rain,
the switchback road, the squeals of our tires, the groan
and clutch of the brakes, the snap and scream inside my ears,
the howl of wind through the mountains that loom
as evil gods who watch us,
her head on my shoulder.
On a high precipice hours past midnight el buso
suddenly stops.

Inside a cave a giant white Virgin blazes
inside two dozen wind-whipped candles.
A half-dozen men circle her,
truck drivers, brown-striped ponchos
rising and falling about their bodies
in the wind like pyramids.

Our driver descends to the roar of their greetings,
stoops, puts money in her slot, lights a candle,
blaze of light! bows, then kneels, prays,

his lips moving
to the white cement.

Now he huddles with them against the Andean cold
into her flame, lights his smoke, laughs
against the abyss far side of the road.
The black moons beneath their eyes
are ghouls over her shine, over the whipped play
of their sinister robes.

Inside the bus I watch, voyeur.
Will I ever understand el hombre?
the masculinity of worship, the pomp of ritual,
the show of arms, the hoard of gold,
the civic idolatry here in wildest nature,
the machismo of their camaraderie,
the kneeling in each's presence to a stone called Mother,
the sex in that

the male spirit of these mountains, volcanoes
spitting ash, this hard
continent, hard driving, my seat broken over the wheel,
my legs aching over our things, my ass, this
rough passage, these tough
passengers, their pungent
smells, oil
of unbathed human leather, spray
of exhaust from holes in the floor, rain
driven through my broken window, our money
in the slot of a virgin. My baby's long legs
out the window all night the bus plunges
the Andes to the sea, to the crying
of an ancient violin

> *vaya con dios mi hijo*
> *vaya con dios mi hija*

b. *Who would dare to find Eurydice?*

Out the window all night the local route
Quevedo, Babahoyo, Milagro, Machala, Santa Rosa, Huaquillas,
dreams emerging from the sleeping
as fairy tales and legends,
as essential local facts.

Inside the window a folding in on myself
a search for legend, the Continental Drift,
the Southern Cross, Eurydice.

¡O Equator, Scales of Love!
that Summer outside
arranges itself
as Winter inside

O collision of the plates, ocean and continent
causing the deep trench of the seafloor
pushing the Andes up

O coriolis, artesian
well all the way up
my eyes

cry
woman, man, north and south
American
the difference a day makes
the direction water spins
down the drain

the offshore wind
coming from all the water in the west
South Pacific, China and Japan
colliding and falling against me
all my life in the Coast Range
Ensenada to Mendocino

now this wind, onshore
from all the land in the southeast
Andes, Amazonas, Brazil, Argentina,
South Atlantic Ocean and Africa
colliding and falling against me
O Orpheus, *don't let me go*

as we descend
the Zodiacal Belt
eight degrees both sides the Torrid Zone
to a desert on the Pacific
"not a drop of rain in two thousand years"
to El Niño, seaboy, *come down*
with me

inside human flesh, divine rivers, O
Americano, Chiclayo, "just remember Chiclets,"
love me until the night collapses, O
genital city, Neruda, coca cola

Love, love, until the night ends
Dawn on her red knees

c. Baja Conmigo, Amor Americano

You come outside our house where I am propped
to fix your car. When you see me
you take out your cock
but become distracted by its scars, white spots.

People gather in the village plaza.
A well-dressed man is begging.
You hand me your plate, your half-eaten food,
instruct: Seek out the beggar, give him
our food. I obey
in love that is not obedience,
but allegiance, our marriage vows.

I'm wandering down to catch him
among the newsmen and soldiers,
the piles of cameras and guns
when I come through the door
awkwardly. Break. As it opens
in four parts
        norte
            este
                sur
                    oeste

Sorry.

Sorry! This insult
for my husband's pleasure.
Our insult of you
to be free of me

from that high northern room
where he masturbates

as I wake
fall back

to your face
face of my true love
graffiti
on the plaza wall

2. My Little Moneychanger

In the morning at the border
between Equador and Perú
the moneychangers surround us
as we descend the all night el buso

to the heat, the screams, smell of dead meat
human piss of Huaquillas.

Mi hija takes their offers, calculates
on her small machine, looks down
in the eyes of each. *Muy*
malo.

Six young men, black suits, black briefcases,
shout back their counter offers.
Again she bends to the gold object in her hand,
fall of her hair, a veil from them.
Calculates, shakes, a spray of gold.
No.

They haggle as we walk
stopping and stumbling
beneath the load of our things
our cramped bus bones
our two blond heads over the dark puddle they make
out-shouting each other,
the heat and dust.
My head pounds from lack of sleep,
lack of coffee, the twelve hour
twelve thousand foot descent.
But my tall Amazon amazes them,
calculates, shakes her head.
No. Nada. She won't be
cheated.

Out the window the moneychangers gather,
watch us eat.
We share a chicken, drink coffee.
Through the window they mime
their offers, play with their cocks,
she counts, licks her lips, taps
—the long graceful dance of her index finger—
her calculator. *Lo*
siento.

In the post office they make their offers again
having trailed us
shouting their deals
the mile-long putrid street.
She raises her left eyebrow, puts her right hand
on her high hip, shakes her wild head,
you must be kidding. Mi little bullfighter
stands her ground.

They make their offers
as we move through customs,
hours through the dust, official papers, silent prayers,
their eyes through the walls of los baños not imaginable,
the filth, the smells, the eyes
on us as we move down the markets, the open stalls,
through the shouts and glares of the merchants, the mothers,
the heat rising with the day, the stink
of the people, the police, the army,
Pasaporte! Pasaporte!
Everyone has warned us,
the books, the signs, the soldiers:
Change your money inside
Equador. WARNING:
Do Not Enter
Perú Without Money!
But my little squirt
my fifteen year old
will not be screwed.

Their numbers grow to see the sight,
now a dozen, now two dozen
come running
to see my girl,
her calculator, her no. no. no.
Little blacksuited men at our waists
gathered in the Huaquillas dust
to make their offers, to play their games
to watch this girl
mi rubia
me too, I suppose,
two giant
electric
light bulbs.

She bends, blinding glitter of bronze.
They peer up, dark and male
collective around her.
Cartagena, Catalina, Galatea.
Her astonishing hands of light
cast the spell of numbers and light.
Her grin, her unabashed love
of this game, center stage,
her poor mama,
all the sexy nuances of nada,
systole and diastole
la señorita si, la señora no.

They know we can't hold out, they see
la señora would have bit
first offer, this dirt in the mouth, headache,
this pain of a place, this dickering
for soles.

Don't worry, she instructs
as we come to the ditch,
the border of Equador and Perú,

as we come to their centuries-old
border war, aching and hot,
the weight of our things,
the guns and the police, guns and the starving
guns and the soldiers
mi hijos, no comprende their cruel
baby faces.

The leader emerges,
the one they ran and got,
the one to whom they all acquiesce, a man
my age. El honcho—they will win
this war yet—sits down
on his haunches. Someone
brings a chair.
Arms across his chest.
He knows
we don't dare cross.

She crosses.
I follow.
Roar of protests,
stench and cadaver of donkey,
stiff legs, a finger to the air,
Equador and Perú,
a naked baby
wandering the ditch
inside outside both countries.
Buzzards each bank, watch,
lift their wings.

The moneychangers get permission,
follow us over. The police,
the armies of both countries,
the bus drivers, the merchants, the buzzards,
women, children and old folks
gather to watch.

And a young woman
we will see all over
Northern Perú,
photograph of a saint,
March 7, 1914
December 29, 1940
stares down
from the immigration wall
through the dusty artificial flowers at her breasts,
the dusted rifles at her brothers' chests.

El hombre makes the offer
mi hija has held out for
all morning, rate of the banks.
She looks at me, winks, looks
him in the eye.
Si (says it so beautifully)
muy bien. Si!
Roar of the crowd.

But, pero, the man
finds he too is in a foreign country,
que lástima! how pitiful
he has no change.
From the crowd, a hush.

So she makes her offer,
my little moneychanger.
Now he is the one
being cheated.
He throws up his hands, I'm afraid
he will cry.

For a kiss, he counters
in Inglés, unbelieving
losing face. Never dreaming
even I

quicker than a calculator
more blinding than God, shocking
even su madre, before he knows
what hit him
mi little conquistador
Goddess, Saint, Banker,
bends to his cheek, smack
of saliva, slipping
los dineros
from his fingers

struts off
vamonos Mom!
with our exchange
to the deafening roar,
soldiers, police, merchants,
creatures they call dogs, buzzards
y los niños
both countries, su madre

following

3. Perú

a. *When you no longer see the trees you are in Perú*

Out the window the Pacific Ocean!
Out the window the orange desert, out the window
El Niño! The mountains loom up like dry bones,
hollow and fainting.

Out the window the heat, the fishing village,
the straw houses woven, pelicans skimming
the wave in a line, seagulls
and white herons thick in a field, following
a man-pulled plow.

Inside Neruda
the nitrous plain, the wastes, the stains
alkali, desert without shadow, desert without time

Village of mud huts where Pizarro landed.
El Dorado shore
strewn with heaps of their garbage.
A three year old sprawled face down at her door.
Our bus backing up to negotiate the curve
around the mud DISCO!
"The only beach in Perú," the Canadian says when we walk it
"warm enough to swim."

Inside this morning when I woke
I was making love to you.
Now I run the Pacific with you
while the breakers crash
the dancers onto the world.

Do you want to have a baby?
                    What
is the Third World?

Inside I carry our daughter here
the way that Indian holds her child,
lets her pull at the nipple
before she wakes and cries
how did I come to this place?

her head in her arms thrown forward on the seat,
annoyed, trying to sleep. Inside
I want to lie my head down on her back.
Inside everyone wants to rest their heads
on my daughter's soul.

     I must tell her of you.
     Of you and me.

         But for me to speak
         is to speak to the lover.
         The lover my muse. El Niño.
         I don't know how to speak
         about the lover

         about you, the men,
         her fathers

         To speak to my daughter
         I must speak of myself
         with you. The self

         I can't see.
         The self she's mirrored

         La Niña
         the self we must stay blind to

         to keep you

Out the window Chan Chan
perfect ruin of dry mud.

the tearlessness of arid skies that never rain.
"You pull yourself up on those walls,
look out over
eight square miles
of a city deserted
six hundred years."

He shows me Chan Chan beads, tiny colored shells.
"The Indians wore them solid up their arms.
The locals have discovered that tourists like beads
so they've been digging up
the burial sites."

Out the window the stone temple of Sechín,
pre-Chavin, about 1500 B.C.
faced with five hundred carved monoliths
depicting battle scenes, men
being eviscerated, heads with blood
gushing from eyes and mouths, dismembered
legs, arms, ears, eyes, vertebrae.
Inside this temple is an earlier temple,
its walls painted of earlier battles.

> *In Chan Chan on the death of each king*
> *his attendant women were sacrificed*
> *buried in a mound together*
> *with his treasure.*
> *One of the smallest mounds*
> *recently yielded*
> *thirteen skeletons of young women*
> *inside one tiny chamber.*
> *The biggest mound contained*
> *the bodies of a thousand.*

The end of modesty is torture.
The end of pornography is murder.
Inside the oldest question of my life
the question I must answer for her

Why the sacrifice of women
in all places
through all time?

How do I speak of you?
Of love?
Of hate and greed?
Of male and female?
Of mother and son?
Of flags and the cross, the
military?

Inside the impossible questions
the obvious
answers, gender
identity, who
besides the lesbians
have answered?

If I try, if I open, if I face
you
to her, my Love

where do the questions lead?
where do I lead her?

To manhatred?

b. Quince

Some days I look at you across the bus
Mama. How surprising to see her here
her unconditional love for me
across time and flesh.

"I'm different than others," you say
against the sea of Perú.
I'm different than others, my mother has always said.

Holding yourselves against sacrifice, prophecy, where
the questions lead. No one, not me,
has the answers you need.

Once upon a time there was a lost little girl,
the first line of all your stories as a little girl.
I couldn't understand, you were in my arms,
in the house I made for you.
But mothers of daughters are daughters of mothers
in circles joined in circles since time began.
My mother wore a mask to nurse me,
afraid of the breath that made her an orphan,
her mother dead when she was three. I've never
been able to see my mother. I've never
been able to see you. Daughter.

Now you sleep beside me on this strangest road
beneath our inheritance, *Capacñan,* this longest
arterial road of history, and the number
rises in me.

I met your father when I was fifteen.
My mother's father died when she was fifteen.
When she was fifteen my mother
ran away from the orphanage.

c. Everyone Warns Us of the Next Country

Outside the Inca road, *Capacñan*
until the nineteenth century
the longest arterial road of history,
three thousand two hundred and fifty miles.

Outside the Sun God weeps
zoomorphic tears:
condorhead tears, snakehead tears.
Inside I weep to realize

I didn't know you were here
each one with your life
each one with your story
each one with your mother, your father, your sister
your brother, your children

your neighbor, your town
your lover, your soul
your earth. Earth's song
to you. Earth's song
of you

>   *how much we love the earth!*
>   *how much we suffer*
>   *to stay here!*

All the days of my life
in my lit up towns
while you were here
in your unlit town

your teeming masses
your Quechua, your
quechismos
on my tongue

pampa, condor, puma, puna,
quinine, llama, alpaca, jerky,
coco cola, tapioca, farina,
gaucho, poncho, chino

as in *his pants, chino*
as in *sweetheart,* you

as in *mi china*
her, *mi*
marvel-of-Perú my

four o'clock
flower, *mi*
guagua

> *The metaphysical fever of the Middle Ages*
> *and the literary delirium surrounding*
> *the novels of knighthood*
> *is still the fervor of the Spanish here,*
> *the architecture, the belief*
> *in El Dorado. . . .*

and cocada

a standard of time
in Perú

the time
during which a wad of coca
is kept in the mouth

about forty-five minutes

d. Demeter in the Long Afternoon

Inside she reads me
Inca: Lover of Gold
points out the window
the Inca ruin.
On its walls
Viva Marx! Viva Lenin! Viva Mao! Viva Ché! Viva Jesus!
history's men who fled their mothers.
Inside the walls
Ceres, Kore, verses
planted in corn

this stepping down the continent
like reading a poem

these days and nights on el buso
investigative poetry
this meditation to understand
this journey into the daughter
this journey to remember
this large girl beside me
like earth in my arms

Out the window a little girl screaming
throwing herself to the ground.
In the doorway her mother, silent, crossing her arms

the son jumping triumphant in the air.
viva el machismo!
leaping breathless
with his father to the bus.
Madre, hermana
cannot go

Outside the longest descent, the endless
ruins, sand dune, the sea, Chimbote

Inca so tall, long boned
black string of hair
Your bus stops nowhere
at nothing
as far as the eye can see, cold
desert without shadow, desert without time

you descend
to your home, a secret

where we will never be found

I see again the drunk Equadorian
in the tavern no woman was meant to be
sitting on the lap of another soldier
inserting his finger into his nose

into his mouth, into his ears, giggling
la boca, drooling
la boca

so sensuous, like a baby unashamed
in love with his mother

like a baby in love with his birth, who
made him
from which he came, the body
in cellular time and earth
the baby
in your arms

> *Men long for us*
> *to find the answer*
> *the riddle*
> *of the Sphinx*
>
> *Men long for us*
> *to redeem*
> *their mothers*
> *against the nightmare*
>
> *adulthood*
>
> *the male forever cut*
> *from his childhood*
>
> *his mother, his*
> *heart, his*
> *womb*

e. Second Night of Pluto

Outside along the road
another altar.
Down the coast another police check.
Inside their cruddy hut
they have been waiting for us,
dos norteamericanas, muchachas
a priest doll, and my girl
beneath the photo of that girl
March 7, 1914; December 20, 1940.
Santa de las hijas, protect us.
Out the tiny crooked window the loaded bus waits,
a puff on the nitrous plain
para dos gringas.

Out the window the white crosses
line the long road to Lima, multitudes
dead in the road, the Pacific
sweeping the dancers off
this world, the sun

off this globe.
We keep descending south, south into night.
Inside some places
are suddenly known

      this is different, this is stranger
      than where we were

the jóvenes gathered on the corners
of mud villages so poor
there is no light
not a candle, not a fire

their mud huts perched
like unseen animals all around the world
ready to pounce

though in this village
the people gather to the blue battery
of a single light, television outside
atop a sawhorse altar

and inside
a couple making love all night
down the coast, down the continent
down the world

f. Ishtar the Wandering Moon

Out the window Orion and my stars
the moment I was born for
this moment of your betrayal

Inside you nail me
at the station of our departure.
Inside my first bus
in San Francisco
I look down
into your eyes
and see

you will not be here
when I return

g. Puberty

We are living in a dry foreign land, Egypt?
searching for my son. Her brother. Daniel.
Somewhere he is playing. A lion. Interpreter
of dreams. I bring in
the bottle of milk from the porch. Mama.
I never understood
those ancient myths. Father. Brother. Son.
Husband. The same
woman.

She is in the living room. Milk
in my arms, she tells me

three days ago a political terrorist
came down out of the hills, machine gunned
her eighth grade graduation class.
Twelve survivors, and they
are badly wounded

She begins to name them, Annie, Denise,
Cory, Kara, Karen, Brandace, Wendy, herself. My tears
break, I didn't know! How

could I not know?

I look into her face for the answer. Sad. But
resigned. Set. Queen
of Erebus. Night
mare. Where

can we run? *But*
she knows

the killer will return.
I know
he has to get them

all

h. Goddess

Out the window the sun rises on the third day
our bus still descending
the coast of Perú

Paramonga   Pasamayo   Chimú

and I see you, Shawn Colleen
walking on the road
brilliant morning
hands in your pockets.
You know where you are going.
I see you, child. One

      I see my mother walking
      a young girl
      the brilliant morning

though no one knows you
The light spinning
off your skin
dazzles us, blinds them, isolates
you

     I see my mother walking

You are so lonely
but
you are walking
to town, oh mi hija, ho!
ha! how you

               O you

walk, oh Mija   Mama
la la
   lalala
        sweet
heart
            You!

you are the road

                         huaca

where you will go

                         O my Lovely

I see my mother
brilliant morning

                         O my Lonely

you are the world

IV. Lima

At length in wrath and in grief
the mother quit the world of the gods,
sat down as an old woman heavily veiled
upon the Well of the Virgin
and grieved.

And continued sitting many days and nights
under the sunlight and moonlight and falling showers.
Her grief was so great
all the Earth began to die.
There was too much sun, there was too much rain,
the birds stole the seed, the cattle died,
the plough broke in the furrow, the seed
failed to come up. Thistles
and brambles were the only growth.

The fountain, Arethusa, interceded for the land.
"Mother," said she, "blame not the land.
It opened unwillingly
to yield passage to your daughter.
I can tell you of her fate.

While I passed through the lower parts of earth
I saw your Persephone.
She was sad
but no longer showing alarm in her countenance.
Her look was as such as becomes a queen—
the Queen of Erebus, the powerful bride
of the Monarch, of the realms of the Dead."

It is the need to enter *what we loosely call the vision to be one with the Imago Mundi, that image of the world we each carry within us as possibility itself.*
—Robert Creeley

Pornography is the end of lust, the final tool of capitalism.
—Susan Griffin

Lima: *The strangest, saddest city thou can'st see.*
—Herman Melville

Lima: *The worst slum in the world.*
—Carl J. Migdail

1. Pluto and Demeter

Descend from the inside, descend
forty-eight hours
inside this bus. Walk
miles through the barriadas
through people who live
on the outside. Through
swollen-bellied babies at your feet who cry for food.
Through children at your legs who beg for your purse.
Through men who look up from their *Playboys* and hiss.
Through their paper huts constructed
with the pages of *Hustler, Penthouse,*
their homes of white female flesh, airblown. Walk
afraid, your sandaled white feet, afraid
your poor poet wealth, afraid
through their piss, your daughter
through their spit, inside through their walls,
pink tits, pouty lips, inside
her vulva, inside every window
a woman
who wants to kill
every man who hisses
this shitty, this deadly
politic.

Inside the pensión in Miraflores
mi niña, my little tourista
mi poca Limeña
turns sixteen. *Dieciseis.*
Out the window the rich jóvenes.
At the door their expensive gifts.
She raises her left eyebrow,
puts her hand on her hip, mi muchacha
mi niñfa, mi china, my little
flirt, my
Playboy Bunny

pooches her lips
sighs
maybe.

Inside I am weary of the world,
made lonely and old by my daughter.
Like the rich boys, I study her,
caught too in the play of hormone,
the divine light
that bounces from her.
I don't understand this world,
the rape of Persephone, the grief of Demeter,
my girl out of me. Where she and I stand
on Earth in time. And men.
Outside and inside, love, this primal war
between men and women
that I fail yet to see, but know in my body
is the only war, the same war
escalated now to the nuclear, that threatens
all of Earth.

Inside the servants hurry from room to room
seeking ways to serve us.
Out the window the children sleep
uncovered on the street, facedown for warmth.
Inside the master stocks his cupboards,
barricades his pensión from the rumors of revolution,
the families of his servants
the millions of starving Indians
coming down out of the Andes
the full length of the country
upon Lima.
Lima "es a small city."

      "I like the relationship
      between you two.
      But how can it be?

In this country the relationship
of mother and daughter is
vertical."

He was born here, inside
comfort, the high quality
of life, he says, the importance
of preserving it.
The vertical and the Sunday ease.
Out the window the birds chirp.
In the suburban street the cars purr. Incredible
the furniture, how deeply
I sleep! I have only to awake
by noon
to be served my breakfast.
I wash her things, her honey stained panties,
mucous of fertility, the llama
sweater, hang them on the line
next to the wet suit, his son's.
A surfboard against the fence.
Inside the washing hut the servants,
mother and daughter, watch me,
whisper.

"An architect, I designed
the post office in Trujillo.
You came through it on the bus, our town
of artists and poets. César Vallejo.
I was born in this house, fifty years ago,
my mother's house.
Now I design these, little Jesuses.
My Indians in my factories in the mountains
make them, little jeSuses, little Incas.
Hear?
They are hand-painted whistles.
I fly next week to Orange, California, do you know
the shopping center? What do you think

of the name of my new shop?
Macchu Picchu"

There are hundreds of ways
to wonder of circumstance
Thorton Wilder muses in the book about Lima
and the road to Cuzco, *The Bridge of San Luis Rey*.
My favorite crucifixion
in the hundreds being packed
hangs above Utah, the town
of my son, her brother,
town from which we began
this journey:

     three inches of Jesus
     above the cross. His head
     floats in space, unattached.
     His heartshaped chest, his legless spine float,
     a soul cut in half. Then his hands
     like birds in air, they too
     fly without visible means
     of attachment

Tonight we hear the news:
the Pope is in Utah.
He says again, women not allowed.
Tonight, very late,
as I come down the hall
past the landlord's room
glimpsing a photograph of a woman who looks like me,
the Argentine German
is standing in his doorway
exposing himself to me.
Both hands, jacking off

     sanctus. sanctus. sanctus.
     Celibacy.

The cause of all suffering, *Buddha says*
is attachment.
Circumcise.
Crucify.
Detach. Objectify. Exile.
Castrate. Decapitate. Deflower.
Uproot. Alienate. Separate. Obliterate.
Segregate. Isolate. Annihilate.
Capitalize.
Rape.

A husband may kill a wife, *Confucius says*
when she disobeys him

history's pitiful men
who float their parts
in the pornographic fantasy
of no attachments

2. Night: Buried America

We don't believe in love
because we don't believe in the soul.

a.

Outside the lust to annihilate
Inside the desire to create

Outside a man dives into the murky waters of Rio's
Guanabara Bay

finds the wreck of a Roman ship
dating from before Jesus
from before Columbus' arrival in the New World
by seventeen hundred years

Inside I see us on our first bed
in the cabin in the Albion woods.
We sit on either side
raise the cup between us
make our marriage vows

You say to me what you love
what you need

I say to you what I love
what I need

But now I see
you betray me

Here I see your lips
to hers, minora and majora
in a loft

You will not tell me
of her
that I might love others
and her

Deception is not
one of the Seven Sins
of your Church

Deception does not count
as one of the Deadly Sins
of your Fathers

b.

Something clangs all night against the house

The oceans move chaotically
across the world
(the Gulf Stream meanders wildly
after leaving
the coast of Cape Hatteras

impossible to predict
how the driven oceans will behave

or the wrath of El Niño
the unruly child
born at Christmas
of the equatorial waters
of Equador and Perú

his warmwater behavior
blowing now through the room
Jesus, Inti Raymi, my Muse

my lover, my son, my southern
oscillation

c. Love Poem to Strong Wind, Amerrique

If I could write the love poem
of my continent to yours
If I could write my love
to you, Strong Wind,
                            Amerrique
dead lips would congregate
throughout the earth and I would tell
of the soul
                        (I would tell
            of sex

as when I stand in the sun
and see the globe of earth
whirl through space from west to east
and see the holy tear
of the South from the North
in the landmass dance
the drift
the removal of his rib for her
Panama
the way they cut you
for speed, commerce

If I could write of this hemisphere
how in love our two continents, the form of our souls
yin and yang, river of mississippi, river of amazon
how her loins articulate the form of all creatures
how we fit
from each other

the way you swing so far to the west, then tighten
your long phallus
in the uterine ecstasy of the chaotic seas
to reach my fat centers,
my high Aconcaqua, my magic Denali

I would blow, Popol Vuh,
El Niño
from Perú to the Bering Sea
the Aleutians' little string
across your Emperor Seamounts
to Russia, Siberia
crumple your islands in the great Gulf
around your sun, bleach
your sands blonde
Caribbean

the way your ocean plates are continually diving down
beneath me

the way Brazil yearns so
for Africa, Aphrodite

       Persephone's vertical descent
       Demeter in her grief wandering horizontally

       this journey backward in time and downward in Earth
       this search for the lost cities, the untraveled,
       this ache for the lost daughters, the unknown
       mothers, this quest
       for the self
       this evolution of the human, holy hejira
       beyond gender identity,
       this return of the fathers
       as Sons to their children
       this search for the Holy Grail
       that contains his essence
       this riding down the world

       like writing a love poem
       my tongue down your body
       this semen   Everyone
       born from the body of a man

this sinking to the ground
this prostration to her revolutions
this touching my face
to her os cervix

untranscendable mold   Everyone
born from the emotional depths
of woman

d. Lima Huaca Birth Dream: Mi Diez y Seis Años

Inside I am running along the beach I raised her on.
The path disappears into the water.
As I climb the palisade to get back
to the road that goes through
I wonder why someone doesn't extend the beach.
Then I wonder why I don't.

I'm in a room with a woman.
We begin to make love. I become a man.
My finger in her vagina. She throbs, contracts,
puts her hand deep inside me.
I am deep inside her.
We hold each other as if we control each other.
Then: the great quaking
conception.

I'm at the gate of this strange city.
I want to go home. My loneliness
unbearable, this journey backward through time.
But she is telling me
the way back to this pensión

Something clangs against it in the wind all night

the servants calling to their families
high in the Andes

Come down, Revolution, come down!
Descend on Lima now!

e. Mama Shawn

> *Why do mothers betray their daughters?*

If I open to you
I'll open to my mother,
I'll open to myself

If I open to you
I'll open to anger
against myself

against my mother

      her tight girlbody against America
      the Cherokee face in the Irish red hair
      against death
      against the New World, love
      against the wilderness

      a North Carolina face

          the Gulf Stream meanders wildly
          after leaving the coast of Cape Hatteras

my mother

who holds herself as if death would come
if the truth were known

my orphan

who holds herself
(because no one else ever has)

who holds herself as if the truth
was death

f. My Girl, Shawn Colleen

My love for my mother

My mother's love for me
has been the only love

My mother was an orphan
a girl when I was born
Her love for me
was for the girl
who died when she was born

I go deaf to protect the little girl inside

I go blind to protect my mother
who has given
body and soul, the world
all the days of her life

I go dumb to hold
the girl

g. Sphinx. The Strangler

My mother couldn't speak

My father couldn't think

My lover didn't know

My country couldn't help it

His lieutenant gave the orders

My son's only road
is away from me

I who can't speak
I who can't hear
I who can't think
I who can't see

h. Oedipus Solved the Riddle of Man and the Sphinx Killed Herself

If I open to you
I will lose my man

If I open to you
I will lose myself

i. Humpty Dumpty

Inside I see you
from the tiny Vermont store
walk the church stone wall
nine years old
beneath the maples of Fall.

I buy bread from the old man
who tells me of his wife, dead.
We both watch you

outside the window
so far from me, little girl
I watch you separate
behind the veil
of colored leaves

Why didn't I reach for you?
What happened to me at nine?

j. Once Upon a Time There Was a Lost Little Girl

I was a mirror in the noon sun.
When she looked at me
my mother went blind.

You are a mirror in the noon sun.
When I look at you

> daughter
> Shawn

the light sears me, the world shatters
I almost see
I go blind

> to protect the rare place
> of wilderness
> the rape place
> Amerrique
> where I'm safe
> as a girl

> you are safe as a girl
> my mother is safe as a girl

I go blind to you to save my mother
my lover
I go deaf to my mother my lover to save my father
I go mute to my father my lover to save myself
I go numb to my sister my brother I go dumb
to my earth to save his world
I go blind to you to save myself
I go blind to you to save you

I go blind like Antigone
to lead the blind,
my father, my brothers

I go blind like Athena
his Goddess of Wisdom
          "For mother is there none.
          I am wholly with the male.
          With my whole soul
          I take the father's side."

I go blind to love
for God
I go blind like Samson
to hold up the world.
I go blind like Oedipus
rather than see

marrying the mother
is marrying the earth

          is freedom

killing the father
is killing the state

          is freedom

3. Patriarchy the Prevailing Religion of the World

Being like maize grains fell
in the inexhaustible store of lost deeds, shoddy
occurrences, from nine to five, to six,
and not one death but many came to each,
each day a little death: dust, maggot, lamp,
drenched in the mire of the suburbs, a little
*   death with fat wings*
entered into each man like a short blade.

a. Maybe Love Was Present Only Among the Poor and Women

Out the window North American tits and politics.
Oil and cocaine equals
inflation, starvation.
Out the window just this year
the economy of Perú:
dope and oil means
the poor can't afford flour.

> *Thirty percent of the protein supply of South America*
> *is from North American cat and dog food.*

Obscenity of poverty the obscenity
of pornography
In the back streets of Lima: *abortions*

> *account for sixty percent of the deaths*
> *of Peruvian women.*

b. The Task of Poetry Is to Overcome Government

In all the store windows are posters of poets.
In all the papers are poems.
Inside I am a North American poet
not honored or read.
In my country poetry: the voice of the alienated.
In this country poetry: the voice of the people.

In my country on the outside, wealth.
On the inside, poverty.

In this country on the outside, poverty.
On the inside, poetry.

c. Inti Raymi

We, the Inca, order and decree that no one shall marry his sister or his mother, nor his first cousin, nor his aunt, nor his niece, nor his kinswoman, nor the grandmother of his child, under penalty of being punished and of having his eyes pulled out ... because only the Inca is allowed to be married to his carnal sister.

Outside the five-year-old girl
who, raped,
birthed a son here in 1939.
The two raised together
as brother and sister.

Lina Medina and her son Gerardo
like the ancient myths
I've never understood

Isis and Osiris
Artemis and Apollo
Raymi and Manko

Oedipus and Jocasta
Oedipus'
self-blinding.

I couldn't understand
men and women.
But now I begin to see

we are born as the child
to the raped child

Now I begin to see,
my son grown,

all men
as their mother's sons.

d. My Mother Couldn't Speak I Can't

You can't say
what you can't remember

You can't remember
what will destroy you

though it lives in you
and you pass it unknown

to your children

making them
the new unknowns

e. Mi Poco Lima

She storms through the city.
Ancient *Rimac*

Astonished I follow
the gold masts
sailing a dark sea
of humanity

through the drizzling fog
the *garúa*

imperious *Mama*   my angry Beatrice

She has brought me this far
beneath the world

and still
I can't open
let fall
the structures of personality and time
my family, my culture

> *(What isn't experienced consciously*
> *can't be remembered*
> *What isn't spoken*
> *becomes the unspeakable*
>
> *I can only parent*
> *what I know*
>
> *I can't parent*
> *what will destroy*
> *the only love I've known*
> *My parents' love. Their*
> *parents'*

At Plaza de Armas
Pizarro
in a glass coffin

and an army tank
colliding with an empty bus

I force myself through
the screams of young men
"Madre! Madre!"
into the next boulevard
a bookstore

Nacida inocente
Sarah

Porno books of ten-year-old girls
next to Franz Kafka's
Metamorphosis

TORTURED WOMEN OF LATIN AMERICA!

and *Playboy, Hustler,*
photos of young women with gaping pudenda
next to the intellectuals, the great writers,
mi presidente

f. La Ultima Conquista de El Angel
(A *Penthouse* Book Review)

Torture is taught by officers
who inculcate students with the belief
torture is absolutely necessary
to obtain information.
There are practical classes, classes
to accustom the students
to torture.
Students never refuse the torture
because then they would be candidates
for torture themselves.
It is made very clear

we must dedicate ourselves totally
to the task to be performed.
What is ordered to be done
must be done.

    •

    The torturer is a special case
    a young man of uncommon susceptibility
    and a searing spiritual ambition

        A doctor is brought to a room
        where she lies ravaged
        under a single light, surrounded
        by police

    •

Our love of the tremulous
of hot and cold peril
draws us to the Chief of the Special Station

a man of dry ice burning inside
reflecting the ominous glitter
of the Andes premonitory stars

who offers us a vision of order
at once civil and celestial
based on a vulnerability
we share

the belief that what is called torture
belongs to a supernatural order
that sanctions and organizes the work.
The Chief is an acolyte to duty,
a godlike artist.

And so we pass in the course of our training
from the servile pole to the omnipotent,

the banality of evil
transfigured by ceremony

carrying us across the threshold
into the mysteries of duty
throughout the chiaroscuro ritual
of the anatomy lesson

.

    After the electric shock torture the only thing one wants
    is a cup of tea or something else to drink.
    I accepted and then they said that after electric shocks
    one cannot ingest any liquid because it may affect the heart.

    The same man who had directed the torture
    and had participated in it
    now spoke to me in a paternal way.

g. *Everybody lost heart, anxiously waiting for death*

The fortune teller comes at me, waving her arms.
I touch her but can't understand
the prophecy she runs off shouting
through the torn and littered park.

At the end of the movie the couple became one.
My daughter said they would be lovers
but when he went into her, she went into him.
Today I am torn and entered by the world.

The bus moans with us, lunges through Lima,
Perú's purple atmosphere, exhaust
and our exhaustion.
Outside they piss into their fountains
lie facedown on their concrete.
On every corner an Indian woman in traditional dress

sells photographs of white girls undressed.
Their babies run after us, begging for our food.
Inside the trees a man leers at me, opens his fly
beneath the little girl on his lap.

The young woman sits at the front of the bus
facing me in the back. The white face
in the dark brush of hair
holds no thought, love, hate or time.
She sits there, blank,
unmarked by prophecy,
our filth and human noise, unentered.
In the bus' groan,
gearing down, stopping, starting up, I'm
hypnotized. *Aymara   Atonement*
I cut my hair like yours

Ten minutes down her boulevard, pure intimacy,
Macchu Picchu lost in the east to all but virgins.
I long to be this girl, not the poet,
torn and entered, not the mother.
To be so self-contained, so calm,
inviolable, impregnable, without protest or dreams,
a miracle.

But *blind Demeter! Fool!*
The girl is so removed from this world
she is falling headfirst from it, a heap now
in the aisle.

When the soldier carries her off in his arms
her legs and head dangle with his red ribbons
like two continents divided
by his uniform.

h. Death Was Born to Her When I Was Born

I sit on the well
and watch you being raped

unable to stop it
to touch myself
raped

> *She sat in silence*
> *watched him take me*
> *watered his grove with her tears*

> *to keep the well open*
> *that I might visit*

> *unable to protect*
> *what was unprotected*
> *in herself*

Psyche's parents obeyed the oracle
her bridal procession her funeral
I wander Earth in search of you
She Who Hides

I hide what I know
deny what I see
don't understand what I hear

Against the blows I get back up
Against the blows I love him

I give you to him
as I was given

I betray you
as I betray myself
as I betray

your brother

the feminine I pledged all his boyhood
as his heritage

to withstand his father
and the world

which I desert
to love the fathers

      O girl
      we are the lost feminine
      the world searches for

      the feminine
      the world dies for

      the feminine
      God
      we are born from

      the Feminine

      Nature

      Death

      the Unknown

      we must return to

      the Feminine
      our fathers betray
      to deny their mothers
      to find their fathers

to find
themselves

to develop
technology

to make
war

the Feminine

our mothers betray
to keep our fathers
to show our brothers

> *though she loved us unconditionally (beyond her own gender*
> *though she combed the earth (all history*
> *and herself desperately (truest Savior*

to not mislove us

> *she handed me over*
> *as she was handed over*

> *as he was handed over*

> *as I hand you over*

though she gave her only body

4. Cojo

He who possesses rhythm possesses the universe

In the middle of the five-way intersection
of Miraflores, Perú,
a man sits all night
working the wild lights of traffic
wheeling around and through him.
He has no legs. *Cojo.*
His job, his gig, how he makes it:
you give
seeing that soon
he will be killed.

When I come to the midnight corner
he looks at me from the asphalt,
from the blinding lights,
the screeching, the honking, the gearing down.

He looks at me.
The way a man looks at a woman.
Shocking me.
Unprepared, unworthy.
I hurry on.

Some nights I'm in one of the cars
racing past a small feral animal
begging for the human food inside our high headlights.
Other nights I walk by him with my daughter.
He looks from me to her and back to me,
his grin expanding enormously
beyond the dark Inca face
into the Andean sky.

This night I come to his intersection
to speak to him, having found

my small courage.
But he is gone.
In the center of the whirling lights
coming from the five directions
is his suit jacket, elegantly laid out.
The gray jacket of his soul left
like a cemetery stone.

I dance all night on the northwest corner,
Discolandia, the nearest station of vigil,
I dance alone
inside Peruvian bourgeoisie, whirling
high heels, aftershave, U.S. polyester,
inside my flying hair, in front of the eyes of a man
who eats by sitting nightly in front of death,
who in the oldest story, a common prayer, a dream
gave half himself to the world,
I dance all night with my prayer, mi jesús,
my legs, his eyes, my leap to the window,
my three inches of Jesus, legless,
my whistle of the cross, my dance
at Eleusis, *don't*
be dead, my poem, *I didn't know*
you were here. I dance alone
beneath the spinning strobe lights
to my North American language, the first I've heard
in months, moving me inside
to the rock n roll, *I ride my llama*
from Perú to Texahama,
the folk music of my land, poetry and beat
stronger than money. I vow in a vision
I don't understand
to cut my hair if he is dead.
I dance him alive

until by morning's first light
I see him in my leap

sitting in the middle of his boulevards
slipping on his coat.
Then his eyes seek me out
as if he's known me here at the window,
my dance marathon, my nightlong prayer and poem
mi epopeya
and makes the circle
with his thumb and middle finger,
nods his head, that grin, *A-*
OK

then slides, in a clearing of the dawn traffic
to the far corner, dust of exhaust rising
from the pant legs he drags, a cloud from him
as the sun rises, through the piss and shit
of the night he missed
and buys breakfast
from the back doors of shops that won't let him in,
with money he has earned other nights
or in the secret adventure of this night,
eats now, propped against *Discolandia*
and looks at me again, grins,
the smile triumphant from the heights and depths of sex
from so far above the war of men and women
I'm carried in his arms
twenty-two thousand feet
up his ancestral land.

5. Mirror

a. Self

For days I've glimpsed her as I've moved down the hall
a photograph of myself
buried in the deep weavings of his room
where his mother birthed him
half a century ago.

Who took it of me?
When was I here before?

Miraflores, Perú.
I enter.
The furniture of Spain drapes the Inca stone. *Rimac.*
The dark hush, the smells of the century
submerge me.

She wears a bridal gown, Victorian.
She stands before her mirror, her eyes
stare back to me.

"Has your face changed?" he asked me in the street
perplexed that I am her mother. "I mean
since you first looked in the mirror."

Her back glows, soul of the world
Rose at her breasts, lost
daughter

Antigua América, novia sumergida

Image of the mirror , the jewel,
lady of beasts, our hair

helios, menstruating
sun

In the flash, Psyche drops the coffin
of divine beauty. One or two stones
split off. My face catches up.

b. La Ultima Conquista de El Angel

I am your face
in the photograph
information
perfume
your mother
Miraflores
Garden
in colors
Petals
Birdsongs
Shroud of your black eyes, masque
of your courage
your lies
woman
in orgasm
depth
of all being
all time
on earth
la ultima conquista
de el Angel, sword
of vagina, womb
of phallus

your brother
your sister
unreceived
in the night of the bed
unrecorded
in the days

of making
world

c. Prayer

Outside the quena reaches yaravi,
her blinding heat.
I touch forward into chaos, break apart
in white aura of hair, shine of her love,
her blinding light
Mama   Mama   Mama

As the urge to the Lord is sexual
As the Beloved is the land
As ecstasy is identity with all existence
As the Muse is a woman in orgasm
As death is Love's accomplishment
As the child is born from the child
As my daughter is my mother
As grief of heart is proof of love, of good
As the forgotten is the forbidden
As the unconscious doesn't know mortality
As we are moved by the world in the ways the
        world moves inside us

let me, as from conception
achieve gnosis, direct contact
with the depth of all Being

let me enter breath
white jade of perfect lake
until all is refracted
is

Daughter

Divine of my Body

Amerrique

6. Mamacocha

Antigua América, novia sumergida

From Lima we enter the sea
wade past the final lips
that break on the shore
till our feet find the land no more.

Now on our backs we turn and float,
our arms let go, our heads, our sex.
The middle parts of us, our souls, let go
and so is arched our hearts
to the twilight sky

and we are turned and turned
by the roar of the land

The Andes settle athwart our hips
then gently turn over upon us
to our bare-stripped hearts.
And reach till they have our hair
and reach till they hold our feet

and we are turned and turned
in their roar
to the earth to the sea to the sky, first star,
Mother and Daughter
past all argument
of the earth

V. The Road to Cuzco

She stood before Arethusa like one stupefied.
Then she turned her chariot toward heaven
and hastened to present herself
before the throne of Jove.

She told the story of her bereavement
and implored Jupiter to interfere
to procure the restitution of her daughter.
Jupiter consented, alarmed
that Earth would die.

There was one condition,
Persephone in her stay in the lower world
must not have eaten any food.
Otherwise, the Fates
forbade her release.

Mercury was sent,
accompanied by Spring
to demand of Pluto
the release of Persephone.

On Friday noon, July the twentieth, 1714, the finest bridge in all Peru broke and precipitated five travelers into the gulf below. This bridge was on the high-road between Lima and Cuzco and hundreds of persons passed over it every day. It had been woven of osier by the Incas more than a century before and visitors to the city were always led out to see it. It was a mere ladder of thin slats swung out over the gorge, with handrails of dried vine. Horses and coaches and chairs had to go down hundreds of feet below and pass over the narrow torrent on rafts, but no one, not even the Viceroy, not even the Archbishop of Lima, had descended with the baggage rather than cross by the famous bridge of San Luis Rey. St. Louis of France himself protected it, by his name and by the little mud church on the further side. The bridge seemed to be among the things that last forever; it was unthinkable that it should break. The moment a Peruvian heard of the accident he signed himself and made a mental calculation as to how recently he had crossed by it and how soon he had intended crossing by it again. People wandered about in a trance-like state, muttering; they had the hallucination of seeing themselves falling into a gulf.

—Thornton Wilder, *The Bridge of San Luis Rey*

1. Ecstasy Is Identity with All Existence

*quise nadar en las más anchas vidas
en las más sueltas desembocaduras*

A year ago today I found Jonathan dead,
this mountain dirt road around his body
drugged, the blue mouth open,
starts up the canyon now into the Andes.
Three days, three nights to Cuzco, the road
to the rest of our lives
in mirror water, in world walking
each mile a shock, as dust flies up
as pieces of heart, tears in the sea, my daughter and I climb
to Macchu Picchu
for the Taurus full moon

Out the window a woman in many skirts, white
stovepipe hat, sits in fields of corn
picking lice from her daughter's black head.
Seagulls swoop to the infant on her back, *Pachamama!*
A white heron watches

He lies there in the road's puddle as he lies on the bed
as I climb to the top of the stairs,
as we climb to the top of these mountains, the road
he has fled for the needle, the bed,
mi amor norteamericano at last
escaped from the world
into the purity of self. (A year ago
on this continent
Jonestown

So I keep moving, giving flesh and organ, son and daughter
opening parts and parts to the violent winds, the lovers,
to all the birthing and dying world, wanting to swim

in the widest of lives, the freest of rivermouths
needing to know all that is fled
by men
their wounded inexistence

2. Queda el Alma

Mama probably cried, mother hardly moaning. Now no one wanted to eat. A delicate spoon, known to me, fit in father's lips, to emerge breaking.
In the brotherly mouths, the entranced bitterness of the son, got stuck.

From Lima to Huancayo, inside the super bus
on Perú's good route
we rock with the red velvet tassels, speed
with our seven drivers
through La Oroya, fork of the Yauli and the Mantaro,
over the thick orange river that slugs
the granite canyon, the smelters, the slag heaps, the company towns,
the women bent to it washing their clothes,
the rocks twenty feet above their heads a burnt stain,
polluted flood. Thirteen
thousand feet

In Concepción
a woman private in her poncho
squats on the corner.
The doors fly open, the children rush on.
"Pan!" "Inca Kola!"
Seven drivers scream, *ha!* yank them from our money,
throw them to the outside, missing the boy
who hides in the back to sell his loaf.

When they see him, his transgression,
they roar, triumphant, slam the door, take off.

We climb. The miles, the clouds splash up,
the towns race by. Now there's snow.
He stands in the aisle, five years old, filthy in rags,
lumpy chopped head lower than the tops of our seats.
Waits. Mucho still. Mucho quiet,

the great human dignity
betrayed only by a bead of sweat
that crawls like lice from the hair
down the side of his long Inca face.

I stare at the drivers, rise, protest.
"Stop. Let him out."
They ignore me, then shrug, then laugh, joke and point.
They have
fun. He can
walk back.
But for the orange shit
the canyon is beautiful.
"Let him out!" They curse. Accelerate.
Their faces contorted, their hatred
unanimous, their foreign
obscenities. *Nadie*
dejó arrullarse,
The boy unmoving in the aisle.
I'm afraid. Where
are we? Do I not
understand?
por su gran calofrío maternal.
Afraid of these men
with my daughter.
We cross the orange river again and again,
gear down and down to climb the canyon of iron,
an ascent, we've been warned, so great
oxygen sometimes is needed. The holy
Mantaro
where the famous actress wrote
aliens live. And the orange
purifying. *She*
bathed in it.

Now after many miles, many villages,
the one who has laughed the loudest,

the one I have shamed the most,
leans to the driver.
We stop in the middle of a bridge.

Without a word, a flinch, the boy
to the great chorus of men's laughter
echoing off the granite, now twilight
walls, descends
to the outside.

Earth.

Now rooftops with crosses, the loved who have died.
Now the river is green, now the river is gone.
Now eighty miles
in an hour.

> Now through the empty corridors
> now through air, land, sea, and night
> comes the human, oh corazón, abused
> face, queda el alma ground small

> > *Walk back*
> > *all the way*
> > *home, you will*
> > *make it*

> > manchankichu, *husband*
> > *out the back window*
> > *flower to Neruda's flower*
> > *all the way down*
> > *the cloudsplashed, pollutedheart*
> > *world*

> > *do not enter your village*
> > *Conception*
> > *a man, enemy*

of your mother

Ama wayqey manchankichu
wayqechallay vulanito
yawar mayu unupiña
rikukuspapas

Ama wayqey manchankichu
wayqechallay vulanito
rumi chiqchi chaupinpiña
rikukuspapas

3. The Bridge of San Luis Rey

But soon we shall die and all memory of those five will have left the earth, and we ourselves shall be loved for awhile and forgotten. But the love will have been enough; all those impulses of love return to the love that made them. Even memory is not necessary for love. There is a land of the living and a land of the dead and the bridge is love, the only survival, the only meaning.

Out the window Huancayo, city of Indians
owned by absentee Europeans.
Oh corazón, oh frente triturada
city of diseased faces.
In the square three men approach us,
talking Quechua, talking confusion
acapana ayápcha.
The scar,
a long slice displacing his face,
cuts his mouth into stars.
Hypnotized, I relive his story
of the knife
as he grabs her bags
as she runs after them.
I watch her disappear
over the ulcerated faces,
beyond the square, into the city, paralysed
to our remaining things,
to this only place for her to return.
Fifteen minutes, a half hour. Longer.
Did I forget to tell her
our things are not important?
What will she do, what will they do
if she catches them?
The images of hell rise within me.
Persephone.
When she finally returns, sobbing,
with trailing children sobbing,
I take her, though I know it's useless,
to the police.

The Huancayo Chief of Police has the identical scar
as the thief. The eyelid cut in half
veils the oldest bridge (the bridge is love), cops
and robbers. Veils this whole town
of diseased faces, karmic,
feudal, political
love, *acapana ayápcha,*
On his finger
the identical wedding ring
I bought her father
in San Diego
when I was her age.
Memory is not necessary, but hypnotized,
I relive the story, the only survival,
all I've forgotten all these years,
the tiny diamond stars
around the silver ring
I slipped onto the finger, most vulnerable,
of my groom

the only meaning. When
they stroke their guns,
separate us, I understand
quick enough to spring back (what he couldn't do, su
corazón, abused
face

they let us go

la madre, su
amor

my arms a ring around her
all the days ride
up the highest road in the world

the spasms of her humiliation
into my heart, my Andean flamingo,
mi llama, mi alpaca, mi vicuña, mi flaminca, mi huaca, mi guagua, mi snow
and rainstorm

       my ex

husband's daughter

> *When I was a girl*
> *there was a girl*
> *from an unknown land*
> *who sang a song*
> *all over my land*
>
> *a song like nothing*
> *ever heard*
> *except inside me*
> *a song that still climbs*
> *five octaves*
> *inside me*
>
> *Yma Sumac was her name,*
> *Andean, Inca, Jew,*
> *my unknown soul*
> *You*
> *mi muchacha, mi*
> *hermana, mi*
> *alma*
>
> *who came from inside me, my*
> *alien, my Unknown, mi*
> *wayqechallay fulanita*
> *mi*
>
> *Yma Sumac*

Out the window the Magnetic Equator.
Out the window the highest continuous road in the world
"rarely dropping below thirteen thousand feet."
Around Pucapampa one of the highest
inhabitable altiplanos,
the rare and highly prized
ash-gray alpaca.

A black-caped, pink-hatted horseman
comes over the purple ridge top
up from the fourth world, a canyon
deep as death. *Cholo*. He canters
the fifteen thousand feet
into blinding silver, Yma Sumac jangle
of howling bells. The clouds
pull back from the peaks, his stallion
dances on them. The sun, *ra-*
mon, pierced by the gaucho hat, sprays
heraldic rays, like a lover coming,
into us. Traveler
for your love.

Yuraq k'anchay maqt'aykiqa
qari saya
Yuraq k'ancha maqtallaqa
chiri angel cholochaqa
qaripuni patikuqcha

We stoop to enter
a dark soggy cave,
the village market.
The eyes of squatting men
are the only points of light,
like stars on her father's finger.
They shine at us.
When we eat the cuy I hear again
Yma Sumac cry and scream

the shinbone of her dead love
yaravi
from the deepest chamber
of the underworld.

¡Lo entiendo todo en dos flautas
y me doy a entender en una quena!
¡Y los demás, me las pelan! . . .

Every other day the bus starts out from Lima
and on the days in between
the bus starts out
from Cuzco
"a one way street."

Now the bus coming down is falling
Now those Germans we met
are dying

Now with every one thousand feet we climb
more coca is legal

the mountains are orphic
what the coca says

far below
on the Nazca plains
in ancient network of lines,
rectangles and squares
whales, condors, monkeys,
"unidentifiable figures,"
and spiders, words
to those
on the stars

a landing strip
to this our planet
of the Weeping Gods

this middle of the night stop
for a woman, a baby on her back.
Where is she going? Where
is she coming from? Chavín.
Mochica, Paracas, Nasca, Tiahuanaco, Chimac. So many

civilizations
all over America
disappeared
just before
we aliens

came. Snowing. The howls
of that baby, my daughter's sobs,
the roof's leaks.
The holes in the floor
spray mud, exhaust
into our mouths, my baby's
nose, crack of the head, color
and bump of the road, mi
bruised totemic, your once perfect face, my
stomach ache, our blond minds
Gringas!
given the broken seat

while the mothers
in the herds of small children, babies
on their backs, always
the baby on the back, the baby
all your life
in the villages of midnight
wait for our bus, wait for the gringas, the neighbors,
travelers, any
hour of night

to buy for less than a penny
the food you make, so good,

so
delicious

I hold her in my arms
though her legs are too long,
though we are here
though it matters not where we are
or it matters for all the universe.
I had to come this far, to this place, Perú,
to hold her

beautiful daughter, beautiful universe,
danger and magic, Andean fiddle, my man
Americano
crazed, a broken tape, and
insignificant, it is

okay, something else
is important, something else about the music
the poetry
yaravi
will keep us at the heights,
Macchu Picchu, city of women, charungos,
femur bones that follows us

five octaves
to Ayacucho, to Abancay

> "They want to know if you are llikichiri
> evil spirits.
> Llikichiri have white skins and blond hair
> and they kill Indians
> to extract the fat
> from their flesh and bones.
> The llikichiri burn the fat in the lamps
> that light their churches.
> So llikichiri must be killed
> in the cruelest possible manner."

We move through Huanto.
At town center
topiary
eight-foot plants carved as animals, llama,
vicuña, alpaca, quanaco, big sad eyes
¡Auquenidos llorosos, almas mias!
circle a woman too beautiful
for words, a plaque, an explanation, a translation.
In the tavern I order cerveza.
He brings me vino.
No one here
understands Spanish.

         Last spring, Edith Lagos, fifteen
         led a massive high school student strike
         in Ayacucho under the auspices
         of a student federation influenced
         by Sendero Luminoso, "the Shining Path"

Ayacucho, in front of the prison
a man through the bus window
pulls my hair
as the soldiers signal
dos muchachas, dos norteamericanas
runs off clutching
my strands in his wild poncho, triumphanting
Quechua
through the line
of school children
who now
as *Chan Colleen* and *Charon Lura*
like the Ephraimites who couldn't pronounce *sh*
descend el buso
to their eyes
their piles of fruit, their piles of guns,
break and run, *shibboleth!*
to touch us

Then in March 1982
came the heaviest confrontations
of this war
in the city of Ayacucho. Two columns
of Sendero Luminoso guerrilla fighters
one hundred and twenty men and women
laid siege to the prison at the north end
of this city of sixty thousand.
Armed with stolen army weapons,
hunting rifles confiscated from rural estates,
and traditional Indian slingshots
to hurl explosive charges
made from the dynamite that abounds in the mountains
the guerrillas overwhelmed
the heavily armed paramilitary police.
Two hundred and fifty prisoners were freed.
Three guerrillas were killed.
In a fit of rage, the police
swept through the city hospital
shooting suspects in their beds.
With this incident
the political situation in the whole of Perú
began to boil

turning around
over an old man
and old woman
falling at our feet
drooling the long river from her mouth
the people!
and nightmares
of culture,
her story, ours
grinning

In September, 1982, Edith Lagos, nineteen,
whose escape from the prison at Ayacucho
had been her fifth
was found murdered
cut up by the bayonets of the paramilitary police.
Authorities called her a leading
querrillera commander in the region. Despite
intimidation and the danger,
the old narrow streets of Ayacucho were filled
by a funeral procession of thirty thousand people,
half the city's population

Outside in the central plaza
Parque Sucre, *huaca,*
the mothers march
wearing black ragged dresses
holding their placards
to the soldiers
¿DONDE ESTAN LOS DESAPARECIDOS?
¿DONDE ESTAN NUESTROS HIJOS?
and in Quechua
Thou Shalt Not Kill

"In the nights the soldiers
pull their sons from their arms"

Out the window La Quinua
site of the battle of Ayacucho, December 9, 1824
which brought Spanish rule
to an end in Perú.
Out the window on the granite cliff
the bus inches around
the names of the Disappeared.
Far below in the ravine, Ayahuacura,
the tortured sons
now being eaten
by wild pigs.

120

Ayahuacura

the name handed down by generations
The Place Where the Dead Hang

Outside the CIA's policy of destabilization, covert
action to create conditions of terror,
proceeds as planned, as with its
thousands of other covert actions.
In the little villages the monteñeros begin to form,
civilian defense patrols, armed vigilantes.
"We are almost ruined with fear," the mayor says.
Articles and photos sent to the outside,
to the papers of my country the day before voting.
Little girls with fingers cut off.
My president calls
for the doubling of aid
to military dictatorships
everywhere. "Ayacucho

the very name
symbolizes
the liberation of South America."

When Jonathan died I dreamed
white polar bears
washing down Topanga Creek to the sea.
Now I dream I'm pregnant with your child
and we live on Topanga Beach.
My children are the children they were then
though you are not the man
I loved then, the man
who loved them.

The sand between our cabin and the sea
is a mountain many storms have built,

an impassable barrier.
We sit on the sand, listen to the Pacific
so near, contemplate
a way over.

My belly hardens.
We hold each other.
We both feel
the child move
between us. Deep inside
I feel my psyche
adapt to another, this
fifth octave, this

child I keep making.

But you say
abortion.
I feel the knife cut
the world inside.

The bus blows a tire.
I walk the two A.M. road,
dirt, shoulderless, lightning
beyond the curve, two thousand feet
above the Apurimac,
Great Speaker. (tell me . . .)
I look down on the village we left
ten hours ago.
Shadow of myself, *giantess!*
against the mountain.
I search the sky for the Southern Cross.
I search the sky for your face, Orpheus.
Inside the bus our daughter dreams

Eurydice
city dressed
squats in high heels

tries to shit
on the road further down.
I know her only in this night
of Southern Hemisphere intimacy,
her beauty, fashion, her
youth, her
shuddering burning farts.
Where is she going
and who in this hell is she?
Hecate above. Abancay,
a night below us,
like jewels
we have forgotten.
The walls of my stomach cramp too,
the birth I keep dreaming,
my love who is dead.
I keep seeing his body on the road,
pool of opium, cloud
of percadine, coca leaf.

The bus takes off without her.
"Wait! You forgot her." Only
my eyes, my
blinding blond curses
llikichiri!
stops
the driver.

She comes aboard, Yma
Sumac cry and scream, *"mi jesús!"*
I climb behind her
over the people
their chickens and stink
to my seat. Sick.
So sick.
But see
mi Chan Chan, mi perfect
ruin, still
sleeps.

Out the window the bridge at San Luis Rey is falling
into the Great Speaker (*tell me* . . .)
The North American writer who came so far
to ask our questions of fate.
I'm trapped in the back seat
by the Indian sitting in front of me
who has let down his seat
onto my lap. I dream
the lice dancing from his hair.
The one beside me
falls to my shoulder, murmurs.
I dream the lice of men, the cramps
of my stomach,
mi diez y seis años
trapped in the opposite corner.

I dream I hold a large girl in my arms,
one hand in her vagina, one
in her golden jungle hair.
She turns into your violin
you haven't been able to play since I left.
I dream I pull you, mi Americano del Norte, mi
hermano, my revolutionary, my
compañero around the curve of earth
and up the shining path, the Andes

but then I find myself outside your house
beneath your window
holding your gun.

4. Edith Lagos Present

Tell me, Great Speaker, Apurimac

A tale told of Shaun or Shem? All Livia's daughtersons. Dark hawks hear us. Night! Night! My ho head halls. I feel as heavy as yonder stone. Tell me of John or Shaun? Who were Shem and Shaun the living sons or daughters of? Night now! Tell me, tell me, tell me, elm! Night night! Telmetale of stem or stone. Besides the rivering waters of, hitherandthithering waters of. Night!

a. *Huaca*

Inside the bus a baby cries
three days, three nights to Cuzco.
Wrapped in her mother's reboza,
held and cooed by her father,
put to the breast, rocked on his knee,
talked to and sung, loved

nothing

will appease her fury, her three day-and-night orgy
of crying, her grief
for being born.
Her screams are a music with Perú's
wail and wang, the driver's tape,
her parents' lullabies, loving ooohs,
the chug and whine of the old engine
up three mountain ranges

until we are descending
the bus in a stop so wild, so high
at the top of the world so wrenched
to every direction, so weird and purple, a painting
would not be believed, the same geography
as the baby's face

and I reach out, touch it
tied to her mother's back
wanting to know her, for her
to know me, wanting her crying
her pain at least
to stop

But she screams then so the mountains shatter,
the uplifts twist, the bowels shudder.
Su madre, so patient, just laughs, runs
bouncing her on her back
down the wet village road.

She is like you, mi hija, when you came
screaming out of me into L.A.,
my wild indignant Russian, my Valentine delivered,
mi Scorpion so angry, so crazed
that November
the sun's longest, hottest reign
broke with rain

That night we went sixty miles across the scorched Basin.
It had been over one hundred degrees for seventy days.
The silent boy drove beneath the premonitory stars,
the long San Gabriel chain, premonitory too,
black and cutting
all the continent to our east.
Deep in our west, our south, our north,
the Pacific churned in from Asia
time's mouth the *Linga Sharira.*
I didn't know
it was the tenth anniversary of my grandmother's death
Lura Maude Edens on whose birthday I was born,
for whom I am named.
I was only beginning to have

knowledge of Earth,
of roads to be taken across her
to her Places.
But *Mija,* mountain
in my mouth, mountain
in my cunt, I will always
be traveling this route,
this time and place, *huaca, eden, plain of sharon*
on which you are always
coming

Just east of downtown we went north
and west again, followed
the underground Los Angeles River, *Porciuncula*
around Elysian and Griffith Parks
circled behind Hollywood through the San Fernando Valley,
dropped back down through Cahuenga Pass
to Sunset, east then

to UCLA

She took my clothes, put me
on that hard board in that tiny green cell,
tied a paper to my neck.
He sat at my feet. Silent. But there.
An occasional grin. The consummate moment
of our teenage marriage.
I had always been told I was beautiful
which made me ugly.
Now I was beautiful.
In the bursting of your coming, muscle, skin, walls,
the paper untied. I leaned back on my hands,
my stretched, engorged breasts exposed, laughed,
entered a strange stream, a sexual
stream, the ecstasy of time and place, a churning

like mountains, like seas at the risen continents.
I could hear time, a machine sound.
I could feel creation, myself in place
for the first time.

The nurse returned, gasped,
tied the smock again to my neck.
When they came, like Gods,
I turned to the wall, rode them out, faults
slipping, upheaval
of spine, of breath, my mouth
to the penciled words at my face,
a woman's art, a life chant, a black woman's
writing on the wall, *shibboleth!*
her labor a bottomless hole into which I was descending
before the sun rose, pain the only world,
the life force, the bearing down, going
back and back before flesh
on the river of all matter
into the body's life, the body's
Mind.

At eight the students arrived for class.
Hija! We were the lesson.
You curled me there, foetal against the wall
as you curled me through the freeways
across the deep and wide basin.
He diagrammed my spine, traced you inside
with his needle, a politic
absurdly outside, so far into you
I had disappeared
from the twenty young men hovered over us
like men over Earth
who think getting you here
is an engineering problem.

b. In the Beginning You Were the Word That Told Me Who I Was

Each cover that lay on us, texture and color,
I still know, the night square
of open window and the images
I hung over the bed.

He was a boy deserted by his parents
who said in the beginning
you are everything I prayed for.

But approaching love
is approaching death. There
on the edge of his answered prayer,
husband, wife, he looked back
to his orphanage, let me fall.

Who can say from out of which body,
which history, which elements
from which galaxy is fear, is courage,
is love made? Or which
of these is not necessary?

You were coming from great distance.
I was a girl planning you.

I came to the bed that night
in possession of perfect math,
moon and her blood tides, the date
of your inconceivable life
and mine, the only moment
and place

of you. On my father's 47th birthday,
Valentine's Day
in a town meaning *Hidden* in a foreign tongue,
one hundred seventeen degrees and five minutes west

129

thirty-three degrees and seven minutes north,
I opened to all your father feared

when he found his mother
when she opened to him

c. The Act of Love   The Facts of Life

To this task I was a woman in the act of love
(her face upturned, her arms around him

the upturning of my body
to you

uterus

universe

existence opening
like a woman in the act of love
the exquisite allowance, the sacred
courage

> *his body of homage turning over to her*
> *his body of homage putting himself into her*
> *their body of homage turning themselves into you*
>
> *his hand to her right thigh*
> *his black head to her white neck*
>
> *this being held down, pinned under*
> *this boy and this girl in the cradle*
> *of the narrow orphanage*
>
> *this rocking on the grave*
> *and resonant lullaby*
> *the eyes and ears of the animals*
> *out the window*

this opening wider and wider
to stone, river, sky, sun
this five-billion-year-old dead star
in submission
this twin cording
all the way back
(all the times and places
they fucked
as there is no
Core, no I
as the layers of the self
peel in absolution
as there is no pinning down

in the ballooning and rising from the cavity
in the walls covered in transudate and clear mucoid

the engorged, erect, deep lurching world
thickened and contracted

her eyes over his
looking directly into the future

the rotating and retracting
the rising
against the floor

this collecting you out of the sensate whole
its eyes and its mouths in continuous orgy
rolling into time out of the spasms of matter
pulling you in and pushing you out
the cradle of blood
waiting inside, a fleshcase
for you to be held in separate awhile
the ineffable elegance and necessity of this act
Earth breathing in
and out in an eight minute cycle
the pulsations and expulsions, the orchestration

(her face upturned to heaven, his body to earth
the contracting in the eight-tenths of a second
beating of the blood, the whole music
breaking full-throated into the ears
the rolling over the top of the wave
pulling all the dead from the trees
the air the rocks the rivers the birds the oceans

the ancient persons

from my side

d. Conception

He fell off me, unable to break
God at his throat.
I lay there a girl next to a sleeping boy
beneath the night open window.
Waited.
Where? Treeshadow, moonshadow,
malebreath beside me.
There in the starshine, breeze, vagina-and-semen smell,
the song of the nightingale

and who?
From out of which moment, which body
which elements from which galaxy
is face, is body, is story, is fate

is personality, is deformity, is disease
is gender made?
Or which of these
is not necessary?

I was to the universe a woman in the act of love
my arms around it, a child
to you. Inside

the suck of uterus. Outside
the star falling through the universe

a girl bringing down into the inside
from out of all the outside
form and content

a certain form
a certain content

to this certain spot on Earth, *huaca*
this boy, this
self

these hands beneath the covers
along side his (that will be yours
beneath the images and the window,
over and over up my body
showing you, pulling you

an hour, two, past
midnight

beyond Valentine's

you were coming from such a far distance
the stone on its way
through star after star

      Then:
      (a moment in time

      you

      a stop, a catch, a yell, an echo, a vow, a yes
      an eruption, most exquisite

      kiss

(my egg
began spinning
in the direction
Earth spins

the Beginning

that rooted me
to Earth

to time and place

forever

e. The Linga Sharira

Dáuín Ní Chaughín Seoin Sean Seoinachine Seonas
Shawnakeen means Storyteller

Your slick, whole body came out of me, screaming.
In the small inner window I saw my mother watching.
In the large outer window a cloud
burst over the city.
The nurse picked you off my belly
where he had thrown you, exasperated
by your fury, held you
to her white cloth, sang
Hush little baby, then gave up,
put you in my arms.

You screamed harder. I soothed your wrenched face.
Cooed. Sang. *Don't you cry.*
You cried so the skies erupted, lightning and thunder.
She took you from me, held you
into his cruel lamps,
what is it, girl?

You've come I thought
from the almond slant of your squinched eyes,
your clenched fists, your blue insane wail,
from the Siberian wastes, the Mongolian plains
of your father's side.
When I put you to my breasts,
the fierce cut of your brow
like a knife from some violence,
I named you Shawn,
out of the blue
from nothing, for no one, not
Darien as I meant.
"But that's Irish for John," my mother objected.
Then the news came through the wall
the president of the United States
has been assassinated.

f. The Word Made Flesh

Your eyes still have the almond slant
of that distant ancestor
the unknown land
Russia
I brought through my body

I bring now
down the world

so like this little Inca
this alien screaming
wayqechallay fulanita

My body turned into your body
my blood turned into milk.
He broke his vow as he made it
but I, poet even then, kept
my word.

Your screams lasted eighteen months.
Nothing could be done
no one could appease you
everyone avoided us
the president had been murdered
but still I believed
in politics, my country
my marriage

Now I see you were alone those nine months
inside with the self I denied
the pain I stuffed when he broke his vow

alone with all that I would protect you from!
(I would kill for you!)
had I understood
you and myself
rather than him

Now I see the child
is the shadow of the marriage
all that is denied

Now I see you are the shocked groom
the rejected bride

the betrayal
birthed, the truth

undeniable
the assassinated president
the foreign country
inside me   enemy

of our country

your screams
the foreign language of my soul

your screams
his soul
all that he made dumb

our screams
our bodies produced as you

to make us hear

your tantrums
to make us see

your screams
a prayer

against every society's
betrayal of the child

5. Father

Psyche travels
life after life my life, station
after station
to be tried

a. *And don't say another word to me / since we can kill perfectly*

When I think of your father now I think of the poet
whose mother died when he was two.
He climbed from his crib
found her on the kitchen floor
lay on her all day
until his father returned
from work that night.

During the wedding the light spilt
like oil from our vows. Burnt, Eden
lost, Eros fled. Now I drive
the night desert, the Mojave
to Death Valley, life after life,
Psyche's first route, her groom
silent, clinging
to the dark passenger side,
crepe paper streaming the Oldsmobile
the night road out of Ramona
dream after dream, my life
north ever since

¿donde esta 'el desaparecido?

circling San Jacinto
furthest exile, highest wall
the summit to which Ramona's husband
climbs in vain to escape

past Big Bear, Lake Arrowhead, Rim of the World
ascending Cajon Pass
through which your grandparents are always coming west
the four hundred and sixty miles
he drove every weekend for two years
so great his love
before the ceremony

I had always promised him
I would drive it on our wedding night

Turning west at the bottom
starting out north across the dry lakes,
through the welcoming upraised arms of Joshua,
valley of El Mirage, mountain of the sidewinder,
past George and Edwards Air Force Bases
where now they land from space
knowing language for the first time
as love

our route a language
to those on the stars
to this our planet
of the Weeping Gods. I tell him

my first stories. *Scheherazade.*
To make him
laugh. To save my life.
To coax him
from the dark corner
he huddles in. *Mi Eros.*
A silence so deep I already know
he will never again
speak.

He loved me
to bring me to the vow.

Now I will keep
the vow, love him
for better or for worse
Drive him, *Oblomov*,
to our first bed

the U.S. Naval Ordnance Test Station
at China Lake
my teenage sailor, my engineer,
his secret clearance, his work
the Sidewinder

against Russia

oh mija . . .

дочь

his father was Russian

that unknown man

who fled his mother, his
birth

the man who is your grandfather
born in Russia, born

our enemy

a man whose boyhood
manchankichu wayqechallay fulanito
was flight from his native home
retreating south with his mother and the army
your great grandfather
General Boris Doubiago, Major General Chief of Staff
of the Tzar's Army

1916 to 1922
south from St. Petersburg
Belorussia, the Ukraine
to Odessa
to Constantinople, to
New York City
retreating

all of childhood
out of birthplace
the infant sprawled across the dead mother
the cold mute land that eternal day
its lost roads, its dying souls, Oblomov
dumb stone of humanity, mythic
landscape, three
generations now

Doubiago

small town on the map
of the Soviet Union
(between Kiev and Chernigov)
deserted home, but home
of generations since

the loss you were born to
the U.S. and the S.U.'s
confusion of property
with place

mi Soviet Union
mi China Lake
mi United States
mi Eden

Doubiago

huaca

God of the Oak Tree

b. Mi Sidewinder

with your eyes
with your eyes of Russia
with your eyes of no money
with your eyes of false China
with your eyes of Aunt Eleanor
with your eyes of starving India

Now I see when he went into me
he shattered
into the shattered heritage of his emigrant parents
into the shattered politics of his two countries
into this apocalypse, the twentieth century

into the child's fear
of losing the woman again
into the psychology of immigrant America,
loss and guilt, (having left, now
stealing, that long day
he lay over her

out of stone, out of star, out of bird, out of river,
out of the grave and resonant music

and ever since I have been Psyche
(Pocahontas, Sacagawea, Evangeline, Ramona, Eve,
Ana Karénina
Doubiago uprooted oak woman wandering
time and the sorrowing continents
picking up his pieces, fear's
fragmented nations

to find you
desaparecida

all that we don't understand
will never
understand

you

God

the Truth

the Living Body

at the end of the world

flower of my youth, my
broken heart, abused
girl, you
hija orgy of my tears, my silent screams
across hell, my answered
prayer

you my unconscious, my best,
my purity, all I denied, the
disappeared
you

child of Psyche and Amor
Joy
child of the human soul
child of human love

you girl of Russia
and the Cherokee

you colleen of America my mother
Scots-Irish
the Seminole, the Choctaw, the Shawnee

Joy!

you Shaun of Siberia
the Ukraine, St. Petersburg, Kiev,
hillgirl of Appalachia, Mama, Moscow

Joy!

you Shawn Colleen
that redheaded Irishman my mother's father
she still searches for

Joy

the vow
the vote
the politic
they can't overthrow
America and Russia
as One

the dialectic
thesis and antithesis,
you Sweetheart
Synthesis

child of California and New York
schizophrenic split, melting pot
all past love
consummated

you my girl my virgin love for him
his fear of love

the murdered president, the raped
present

you loss of my virginity, materialism
of his ejaculation,
Self-treason. My treason
against America. *Zhivago!*
when he went inside me

you, Soul of the Other
born out of me
you the inside of the outside
Oblomov
flight of
his boyhood, his nation he conspired
with the enemy
to destroy

this Inca screaming
God at the throat
this Sphinx the Strangler
the knotted tongue, the

Word

loosed from all flesh
all land
Africa from Aphrodite, cocaine
from coca cola, mother
from mater, vote
from vow

you
the journey Psyche makes
all the roads

that I love

for loss of him

in pursuit of him

to find you

lost *huaca*

>you who I loved
>for loss of my name
>*Sharon Lura Edens*
>
>you who I loved
>for loss of my mother
>*Audrey Garnet Clarke*
>
>you who I loved
>for her loss
>
>her mother
>*Susie Simmons*
>her father
>*Guy Clarke*
>
>you who I loved
>for the loss
>of Russia. *Doubiago.* His
>father
>
>you who I loved
>for birthing his son first
>he who I raised
>to be a man, that is
>
>to hate me

you who I loved
for loss of you, unknown

daughter, lost
little girl

you who I love

the girl I couldn't see
the orphan, my mother, the girl
I couldn't be, Earth's
true martyred one, true

Christ

who finally stopped screaming
when I left him

you the girl I nursed
while I read
War and Peace

you the girl of the boy of the U.S. Navy
you the girl of the navy wife
maker of weapons against your heritage
geology of flesh and blood, girl of my first boy
computer whiz, electronic
engineer, underpaid
worker
of holocaust, radiation
apocalypse

you our politic

you

our karma

6. Nuestro Ché: The Monroe Doctrine

All night armies of people and your guerrillas
across my face, an epic poem.
I fall in love the month they kill you.
All night I fall through the Andes,
into you in Bolivia. Into Indians, almas mias
you couldn't understand

All night I take the shapes of older stories
Psyche in her transmigrations
a power struggle on that sunken continent
in which I use the people as pawns
three thousand years of bodies and bodies
hysteria in every one I create
and every one I lose so violently.
I take a female body and lose control
become their oracle in my violent trancing
yes, yes! I was murdered.
In all my lives I am assassinated.
When I wake to this bus climbing the Andes
my daughter is in the window
beyond three Indians writing in her diary.
I call to her
I love you

then fall back with you in Buenos Aires, Guatemala,
the secret Bolivian valley where we train.
All night I wake and call to her
I love you   I love you

and dream the words I love you *streaming with light*
through the holes in your clothes,
see in a vision the epic structure:
the beautiful globe of blood-streaked earth
whirling through space from left to right.

All night you tell me you are throwing yourself
upon the world, riding the tossed coin down.
It isn't living or dying but being altogether in love
with the turning of the world
into darkness, into light. When I wake
my daughter is a dark image
on the bus window, the women on my mother's side
Cherokee, Seminole, Choctaw, Shawnee
all my fathers' revolutionaries who gave up everything
for love, for the turning of the world, squaw
and their nations the only names
on the marriage certificates.

All last year I sought America
traveling with you across their continent.
Now I search with our daughter down this one.
You said the Andes are the feminine part of Earth
and a revolutionary is motivated by feelings of love.
You said like all revolutionaries
you received your politics from your mother.
All night I write the love poem of North America
to South America
because the first time I saw you Love
I saw my death, the presidents

at your mother, those idiots
at the bride's door. All night
I see the body of my beloved
dismembered in waking, Monroe
coming through the walls of the Andes
throwing herself upon me. Yes! she cries
causing them to break, write it!
You must write the American poem.
I was murdered. I knew too much
about Cuba, the plot to kill
Fidel Castro.

The Army is around us now with their raptures of Armageddon,
their liquid red crystals that see through the night.
I can't understand what being pretty has to do with the Revolution.
I'm murdered because I love you.
Psyche is immortality but you who are human love
attain the inhuman unforgivable calm of your last days,
giving up the burden of your personality, riding
the tossed coin down.
You put yourself in the keeping of the Indians,
are whatever they say you are. If ever
we birth our child she shall be Joy, but now
you don't speak yourself, they
speak you. When I confess

my betrayal that first time so long ago of the people
you are like them. You can't forgive me. You cry
you will betray me again. O mi Amor, mi
compañero, I vow
my love is eternal, I give up
the burden of my famous body, I'll be
whatever you or they say.
I won't speak myself anymore, you
speak me.

            All day I listen to the birdsongs
            for the lost languages, study the maps
            for the tiny villages where we spoke
            where we fled the CIA's policy
            of covert action and destabilization
            All night the helicopter is flying
            from La Hiquera to Vallegrande
            with your corpse tied to a board
            across its runners

            And then as is their custom
            with the dead bodies of guerrilleros
            the Army is putting you on display
            across two sawhorses next to a shed

150

with a red tile roof and no front wall
in the middle of a dusty field

Then at dusk some Indians come
place candles at your head and feet
They kick the sawhorses that you lay on, pray
Now every evening they come from their fields
in ever increasing numbers. So the soldiers
take you away, cut off your hands, stick them
in a jar, load you onto a small plane
and throw you into a jungle
where no one ever goes or goes
and comes out sane

All night through the Andes I bargain with you
clothed now in the glory of their violence,
my daughter, my love poem to the continent.
All night I so love the world, riding the tossed coin down
this foreign road
I display myself

my unforgivable crime of love, your oracle
your eternal punishment of me, my martyrdom

        your feet wrapt in filthy rags and pages of my diary
        the wings of condors on your back
        a rifle in one of your bloody hands

my oracle, your martyrdom

        my body returned home
        after I am already dead
        my heart broken where you injected the needle
        stole my red diary
        where I wrote for all the ages
        my epic poem
        I love you, I love you

Even the coroner that we share, love
he who is not from America
testifies

you murdered me
los hijos, los hijos Amerrique

VI. Cuzco

The wily monarch consented.
But alas! The maiden had taken
a pomegranate which Pluto offered her
and had sucked the sweet pulp
from a few of the seeds.

This prevented her complete release
but a compromise was made.
She was to pass half the time with her mother
and the rest with her husband Pluto.

Cuzco was shaped in the form of a majestic puma which lay on the dry bed of the primeval lake Inkill. Its stone head rested on Hawks' Hill and was formed by the fortress of Saqsaywaman. The outline of the first wall of the plaza represented its pointed fangs, while its blazing eyes were the towers faced with gold sheets, shining in the sun.

Over the great back, there still runs the Tullumayo, called the "river of bones" because it wet the backbone of the god, whose velvet-sheathed claws closed on another ancient river, the Saphi, "the fountain head of springs." Its tail ended in a street which still keeps its old Indian name, Pumaq Chupan (Puma's Tail).

Thus the city itself was an idol and the inhabitants of Tawantinsuyu, before entering it, knelt to do homage, their hearts swelling with joy. The mere fact of having been to Cuzco, says Inka Garcilaso de la Vega, was something so extraordinary that if two Indians of the same class met on one of the roads, the one coming from Cuzco was respected and revered as superior, just because he had seen it.

The puma city was a temple to time, a calendar city which reflected in the careful geometry of its streets the universe with its planets and stars. The seasons were represented in the symbolic grouping of the four suyus bordered by the main roads which started out from the sacred plaza of Waqaypata to the four regions of the Empire. Its twelve districts represented the twelve months and were counted clockwise. Each district had three main streets and each of these was equivalent to a week of ten days. The first was called Qollana, the second Payan and the third Kayao. Each day was dedicated to a god and therefore there were almost three hundred and sixty-five huacas to regulate the march of time, ruling the elements and the life of men.

—Alfonsina Barrionuevo, *Cuzco, Magic City*

1. Parthenogenesis Baby in Stone

Yo hatch katchkani
Manan yo hatch katchkani
Chaimita tapukui

To be
Or not to be
That is the question

In the first hours of Cuzco
I fell asleep
and dreamed a baby
as a test.
I didn't know then
the soul of Perú is a stone
but I saw that I could wake
and show you
how the human comes
to this world.

I was placing the baby on the ground, leaning
the Goddess over it. Speaking.
The baby contracted
into an emerald.
Then spun, geometry, the sun,
a whirl of rainbows, precious
stones.

Again, I put the baby on the green tile floor
and climbed over it. Alchemist. Cooed. *Mi quipu.*
The infant opened its eyes to me
and cooed—smallest, brightest.
Incorruptible. Rock of it.
Then spun back around
to the world, breath and flesh,
larger, more vague.
Soul.

My son!
just as he came
out of me

so happy, the rock of him!
How he loved to be loved, the soul of him!
Then tears, the growth of him.
This made me cry. Cuzco. Betrayal
of him.

And dizzy. *Soroche*.
When I woke I felt the earth
quaking. His sister beside me in the bed,
snoring. Breath
of the hard world
in the high altitude.

2. Once Upon a Time There Was a Lost Little Girl

I climbed down the ladder to you on the beach
playing in your bikini and scarves
with the wind and the waves, your ballet
in the rigging of the beached catamaran.
I began to play, a girl myself, and found you,
all your six years, in a crash of water
upon the world. *Amerrique!* I was
the wild wind
to see I had almost missed you, so in love
I was with him, *mi esposo.*

My mother told me many times
as if a warning against the natural
a woman must put her man first
before her children. And you
were so in love with him
which we all understood
as natural. We lived on that beach
to escape the unnatural city,
its dazzling white skyscrapers
rising like ruins on the bay to the south
but some of the truths of human nature,
of mother and child, of woman and man,
remained out of reach

though now, like some sudden change
in the weather, Santa Ana,
earthquake, the grunion
running on the spring night tide, I was
free of him, his nature.
I'd put his things on the patio, left the note.
We lay on our bare bellies in the hot sand,
our heads to a circle of the female, sifting
ground shells through our fingers,

making piles and, *sweetheart!*
I discovered you! Amazed—*he had been*
a blind between us!—I said
some things a mother could say
to her daughter. I rubbed your back
with oil, turning you
gold.

But then he returned.
I felt him up there
discovering his things.
Women understand men
because they birth and raise sons.
But they fail to understand their lovers
as the sons of daughters. I thought I was loving you
by loving him.

His week of cruelty turned to charm.
I climbed back up the ladder, the moment
I married him. You

I see only now

wandered down the beach at low tide
the self my mother lost to keep my father
the fog moving in with the setting sun.

3. The Soul of Cuzco Is a Stone

a. Darling Shawn Colleen, a Girl

Beautiful, beautiful, beautiful, beautiful
girl

Out the window Cuzco! Eleven thousand feet
Spanish capital built on the Inca ruins.
Out the window coca trees, stone walls, a parade
through the plaza, November One,
Day of the Dead, headstones
whitewashed, babies
made of bread

Out the window the Death of the Last Inca
Out the window Dia de Guerrillero Heróica
Out the window the day Ché Quevarra died
Out the window guns and bombs in La Paz

Out the window the Black Jesus
the mestizo Son of God
is carried on your shoulders
Taitacha Temblores, Viraqocha Tembloresman
Lord of the Earthquakes,

> *when*
> *wilt thou redeem the pain*
> *of one race*
> *by another undone?*

Out the window, *ladrón!*
the bag on my back slashed,
thieves in the market place.
Old women screeching at me, their pockets
full of coca leaves.

Out the window the legendary land of Pacarectanpu

A llama steps delicately down
one hundred Inca steps
the pink tassel in its pierced ear swinging on the sky

led by a young girl whose thousand braids
swish beneath her red, pieplate hat,
its thousand tassels.
A tiny baby asleep
in the reboza on her back

> *Before you go to sleep*
> *say a little prayer*
> *Everyday, in every way*
> *it's getting better*

Inside mi Shawn Colleen sleeps
soroche, altitude sickness.
Even the coca tea
the manager serves
regularly, legally
has no effect

> *Darling, darling, darling, darling*
> *Shawn*
> *Darling Shawn, see you*
> *in the morning*

b. Pacarectanpu

From out the Three Windows of Stone, Tanpu T'oqo
by order of Teqsi Viraqocha
came eight gods one day
full of power and wisdom.
The men were called Ayar Manka, Ayar Awka,
Ayar Kachi and Ayar Uchu.
The women were called Mama Wako, Mama Oqllo,
Mama Ipakura and Mama Rawa.

None of them had either father or mother.
Their mission was to lead the people
and form a great empire
whose capital would be the place
the golden rod they carried
buried itself in the ground.

As they succeeded in their task
they were turned, one by one, into stone.
It was Ayar Awka who first entered the valley of Cuzco
carrying the golden rod
which instantly
sank into the ground and he into stone.
So the place was called
Ayar Awka Qosqo Wank'a
which means
Ayar Awka, the Marble Boundary Marker.

From the land itself, from the beginning of Time
came the decree:
The Empire must not be divided.
But outside time
Wayna Qhapaq divides the Inca Empire between his two sons
Atahualpa in Quito, Huascar in Qosqo,
the last two rulers before the Fall.

c. *In the land of Pacarectanpu living coffins*
wander at midnight in search of their corpses

Out these Three Windows of Stone, Tanpu T'oqo:
God's city

Outside the head of a mythical puma
emerging from the ruins
his fangs bared between the Tullumaya and the Saphi,
the moon held in his gullet

161

Outside Qorikancha
The Golden Enclosure
erected by the first Inca, Manko Qhapaq
and his harem of sister-wives
the most extraordinary building
of pre-Spanish America

Temple of Birth and Death
The Beginning and the End

its sanctuaries
of the Sun, Moon, Lightning and Rainbow
surrounding the Inti Pampa, the Field of the Sun
in which llamas of solid gold
graze on golden stalks
of grass

Outside the builders turn to stone,
the stones turn to warriors, the
puran runa
In the Square of Joy, Kusipata,
the stone of the soul of a woman

the beautiful Inkill Chumpi
who saved her people in P'isaq
but when she looked back
to the prince she loved, Asto Rimaq
she turned to stone

Outside lining the tops of the walls
of Pachakuteq and Wayna Qhapaq
spears
on the points of which stare
the heads of their enemies

Outside in the Square of Weeping, Waqaypata
drums made of the defeated chieftains
whose hands are the mummified sticks

that beat their empty bellies
whose throbbings come
from their open mouths

Outside as Atahualpa prepares his entry into Cuzco
having defeated Huascar
after five years of fratricidal war
Pizarro lands
with his small army at Tumbes

Outside in the plaza at Cajamarca
Atahualpa is carried on his litter
to greet the gods, half-men, half-horse
who have come from out of the hatuncocha

and the cannon belches out its thunder
and the Spanish give their cry
"Santiago and at them!"

and the people of Cuzco
prepare to meet their liberators

Outside in the Square of Weeping
the breasts of the women who supported the rebels
when Manko lost the city
cut off by the Spaniards

turn to stone

Outside eleven thousand llamas
each loaded with one hundred pounds of gold
to pay the ransom for Atahualpa
setting off across the high plateaus in caravan
never to reach their destination

Outside seven hundred sheets of gold
a finger thick

from Qorikancha
in the bottom of the holds of galleons
on the way to Spain
even before the main body of Conquistadors arrive
to change the Western World
from feudalism to capitalism

Outside the golden statues of the Inca kings
each the size of a twelve-year-old child
that Maria Esquivel was shown
after a blindfolded journey
by her husband Cristobal Paullu Inka
grandson of Whayna Qhapaq

and the main garden of Qorikancha
four thousand loads of silver and gold
hidden in the immense underground vaults
near Saqsaywaman

a generation will not reveal
in their lives of prison and torture
the secrets buried with them

as Tupaq Amaru
the last reigning Inca
makes his raids on Cuzco
from Vilcabamba, from
Macchu Picchu

Out the window the mountains are stone condors.
The people read the coca leaves,
take revenge against their subjugators
with cocaine, watch
the Spanish bull
fight the Inca condor, await
the future raids
of Tupaq Amaru.

On the lonely roads the nak'aq
assassins unsuspecting travelers. Juan Oso
births from the union of an Indian girl
and a black bear,
destroys forever the white man's hell.
On a single pyre, Inkari, the avenger,
immolates all those who do not speak
the language of the people,
runa sumi

Outside below the weight of the foreign gods,
Jesus Christ! Conquistador!
Santiago! Killer of Indians!
the native sandals trail
giving the illusion they are carrying
their deaths on their shoulders

but beneath the voluminous silks
they place *huacas,*
carved Sorcerer Christs
who crucify Spaniards

Out the window
the Wandering Virgin of Quito,
the Virgin of Cocharcas,
the Conquering Virgin of Bethlehem,
the Virgin of Koka Akulli, the Virgin of Descent,
the Mestizo Virgin, the Indian Virgin, the Mother Virgin,
the Mamachas, their famous earspoons,
their splendor of choclos, chupetes, caravanas
of pearls, rubies, diamonds and emeralds,
their embroidered dresses, so many petticoats
with precious lace flounces.
Out the window
Mamakilla
wife of the Sun and Queen of the Night

4. El Machismo

Descend the pink cobblestone street
"Hey Jude," from the turquoise windows
high in the adobe, thirty ten-year-old boys
singing down to Shawn
"don't let me down!"

A boy in a uniform blocks our way,
soldier or cop? Gun
on his hip, machine gun
in his hands, his beautiful hands,
the beautiful sound of typing
from that window, the funny
Hare Krishnas

> *Kṛṣṇa Kṛṣṇa,*
>
> *Hare hare*

"I like them," she says
"They're different. They make me
laugh."

In the Square of Joy
an old man ranting at us,
slime and pumpkin seeds
awash his knotted arms, his muddy face.
An old woman hexing us,
her muddy rags, her bare feet.
Tiny white dots for eyes.

The quickstep walk of the Indians,
a pigeon tiptoed shuffle.
The way they were bound as babies?
Arms wrapped tight to the body,
the heavy loads they carry
on their backs?

Stick step, stick gesture
the peasant's function,
function of silent
strength and of burning bush
the word hanging from another stick

and their chests like barrels.
Room to breathe
in the high air

Inside one shop on the Day of the Dead
The Grateful Dead, *you know our love*
won't fade away.
You know our love
won't fade away

Inside all the shops on all the walls
the naked women are blond
the pouty swollen sunburnt lips.
"Our love," he explains, "of rubias."
In *The Snackbar* we drink cocoa.
On his knees, a boy sings to her
the Rolling Stones
I first heard the night she was born,
"Under my thumb, the girl
has become. . . ."

while another competes
Van Morrison
"So hard to find my way
Now that I'm on my own.
Saw you the other day
My.
How you have grown."

"I know people," the bearded gringo exclaims,
huddled in the corner

167

beneath the poster of her wide opened cunt
sipping tea, reading Kerouac
On the Road
"who've never recovered
from this trip."
He's from Seattle, fighting
dysentery.

"You.

My brown eyed girl."

The newspaper headlines scream
GOLPE EN BOLIVIA!
So I ask him
about the many revolutions,
seventy-three since winning independence from Spain
in 1825, and this time,
a woman is made president.
"In Bolivia they are really
just military coups. Guys
fighting for power. Behind them
are their mothers.
Then the students. Then
the miners."

"Matriarchies," he goes on, "always produce
military dictatorships. The sons
trying to wrest the power
from their moms."

He was planning to return
so he didn't change his money.
"Now, this paper,"
and he lights his pesos,
"is shit." The beggar kids
stare.

"The white hat women," he says, "are mixed.
Spanish and Indian.
The round hat women,
Indian.
When they get married
they put things in the hat."

At the University of Cuzco
the most popular major
for even the Communists
is *Tourism. O
domino!*
The jóvenes study American films
for their parts. They run at us
as old movies rerun

the goon, the punk, the surfer, the motorcycle kid,
the hippie, the farmer, the banker, the playboy, the cowboy,
the bad guy, the president, the thief, the all-American kid

One boy approaches
as we walk the plaza
a bookie from Brooklyn

Bob Dylan
scuffs by
*"I long to see you
in the morning light"*

Over and over *madre y hija?*
No hermanas?
This guy says, authoritatively,
to her of me, in Father's voice,
"She
is your brother."

Outside the faces of the children who beg,
heads all tilted to one side, hands out
so sorrowful.
The maudlin look
taught by the mothers.

"Brown Sugar.
Just like a young girl should"

Outside in the Square of Weeping
a ragged six-year-old boy
ties with a rag
a ragged two-year-old girl
to his back

In the Macho Pizza
a boy constructs Jacob's Ladder,
string on his fingers.
We give him the piece.
He leaves us the string in trade.

Outside a man, his five-year-old boy, pass,
then stop on the crowded walk.
The father turns the son around
points at mi hija's ass,
instructs
the boy in what to like, how to
zz-zzzzzzzz!
a man

Inside this mother
flies around
glare and curse
Zz-zzzzzzzz! back

Outside the Indian student
majoring in Communism
who begged to make love to me

hurries by, Gorki's *Mi Madre*
in his poncho

"Your eyes! Your eyes!"
A taxi full of guys.
"Gringas!"

"Excuse me
while
I kiss the sky!"

"I feel a lot of tears
behind your struggle,"
he whispers from behind, *"Let me*
step into your fire."

"I'm sick of these guys!" she breaks.
"I wish they'd leave us alone!"

> But these guys
> are not concerned
> with us.

> When they stand at our faces
> rapaciously staring
> they even pretend
> their oldest buddy
> standing right beside them
> rapaciously staring
> isn't there.

In Waqaypata, Square of Weeping
now Plaza de Armas
we look for Powhatten
North American headfeathers and moccasins,
father of Pocahontas
"shipped here by mistake a hundred years ago."

I quote to her, mi India,
as he addressed the Whites

Why will you take by force
what you may obtain by love?

I tell her the Cherokees walked north
perhaps from here.
I tell her the story of Mormon
who walked for twenty years
north from Cuzco
two thousand years ago
writing all the way.
He saw not a "living soul,"
recorded only the silent ruins, the empty cities,
luminous, perfect works of stone,
the land spewing ash and terrible piles
of human bone

until he arrived in what is now
New York State
buried the writing
on the hill at Commorah, the story
of his lost civilization

and this is why some believe
the two continents are holy.
Volumes, whole libraries, like the Inca gold,
are buried in it. The written word
inside the land

Out the window on the world's highest lake
Titicaca, people who never set foot on land
but live in boats and ceaselessly cruise
the giant lake for food

Is cocoa
sweetened, chocolate-flavored coca?
What does *Andes* mean?
Andean, Indian, Eden, *Brown*
Sugah . . .
Just like
a young girl should

do you remember when
we used to sing
shala-lalalala?
shala-lala-lala,
la di da?

you
my green eyed girl

5. Saqsaywaman

The pucara *of Cuzco ... one of the greatest structures ever reared by man.*

If coca did not exist—neither would Peru.

Some historians think that the fortress was built by Titans who molded the stone in their hands ... since they did not need to cut or work the stones. The giant blocks fit into each other so perfectly it is impossible to insert the blade of a razor between them.

Or perhaps it was
that the stone itself
found the will
to tear from the hearts of the quarries
to travel
over rivers of human bodies, defying horizons
through half a century of imperial
suns and moons.

In this epic of cyclopean stones
there were some like the *saikusqa*
the tired stone
that traveled forty-five miles from Yukay
and fell, exhausted,
halfway up the hill
crushing thousands of men.
There it is to this day, sunk in the earth,
still weeping tears of blood
for grief at not arriving
to Saqsaywaman.

And here is the stone head of the puma
these two towers
its eyes
rising to the sun
in which the soldiers lodged.

The third tower is its muzzle
in which the Inca Sapa stayed
when he visited the fortress
the rooms faced with sheets
of gold and silver
through which ran
a spring of clear water

from which Manko II
threw himself
rather than be taken alive by the Spaniards.
He had fled to Saqsaywaman
spurred by his sister-wife
Qori Oqllo, *Seed of Gold*
to win back Cuzco.
When he saw all was lost
he wrapped himself in his cloak
and threw himself from the two hundred feet.
Pedro Pizarro witnessed Manko
like a lion, like the greatest of Romans
killing his own Indians by his fall.

Out the window
the underground tunnel
two thousand miles through the Andino spine
Cuzco to Quito

The Mormon missionary takes us down
the dark two-foot entrance. "Now
there is not even a road
from Cuzco to Quito.

Down here the Incas
buried their tons of silver and gold.
Many have entered at Cuzco or Quito
but only one ever returned.
He spent ten days wandering
beneath Cuzco, came out

holding a golden ear of corn.
But he was mad.

The Mormons believe
the tunnel is full of writing.
When they knew their world would be destroyed
the king spent all the last days
trying to speak to the people.
But every time he opened his mouth
books emerged. Though scholars say
the Incas didn't write."

We slide down
the Inca slide. "Si," Juan says, "they were
crazy. Too much
coca leaves."

> *The secret of their success*
> *was their fetish for organization*
> *enforced with an often*
> *bloody ferocity*

                    Fascist
in the blood," Carlos says. "Coca
built these walls"

and underground passages
of so many streets and side-turnings
that even then "those who knew it well,"
the Inka Garcilaso wrote
"did not dare to enter
without a guide."

And here in the second wall of the East
is the stone with the soul of a woman.
Hear how she cries when struck,
a clear limpid voice

murmur of a dove
imprisoned in the rock.
Saqsaywaman!
She answers to anyone who calls.

Saqsaywaman!
Her wall bulging in and out like a dress.
Saqsaywaman like Demeter's Laughless Rock
Saqsaywaman I keep asking Juan
how do you say it?

"Saq say waman
Saq say waman"

But each time I hear
flesh, blood, soul, and song
mi jesus, mi hija, mi
Yma Sumac, her
saxophone
slamming

sex say woman
sex is a woman
sex a woman, sack
a woman
sexy
woman

wo
man
woe the man, woe

the womb man

"Saqsaywaman!" Juan laughs
"Saqsaywaman means

Satisfy the Fool!"

6. Jesus Viraqocha Tembloresman Mi Jesus Presente

Viraqocha, Lord of the Universe
Whether male or female
Anyway, commander of warmth and generation
Being one who
Even with your spittle can work magic,

Where are you?

Inside the cathedral Cristo de Negrido.
"Real Inca hair"
robes the black torso
to the black bony knees. Bells
tied to his nail holes.
Ancha sumac Taita most beautiful
Lord of the Earthquakes,
Taitache Temblores. March 31, 1650. May 21, 1950,
four hundred earth tremors
in twenty-four hours, the people
dying on his cross.

Inside the cathedral Jesus dead
dressed in a pink lace gown
laid in a silver glass coffin,
Made in L.A.

Jesus in their diamond rosettes, strings
of ten and twenty thousand pearls from the East
hanging from his neck

Jesus hanging out his gold undergarments,
his slippers and crowns, his Inca tunic
to dry on their clothesline. Gold.
And gold clothespins.
His countless capes of fine brocade, set

with precious stones.
His countless embroidered dresses, rose clouds
of tulle, diamonds set
in platinum, brooches
of flesh and flamingoes, a whole
people
hanging on his line

Jesus in his gold, *sweat of the sun*
Jesus in his silver, *tears of the moon*
Jesus in his rubies and nuqchu vines
passion flowers
bleeding from his wounds

> Jesus, Lord of the Storms (your
> sixteenth-century voyage from Spain), most
> kindly Lord. A toy, the U.S. Naval ship,
> carried in your bosom. And Raphael
> your angel, holding with love
> the big fish
> to your heart

> Jesus my son
> on whom they hang their sports medals
> holding up a gold-framed photo
> of yourself

> á mi mocha, my
> ceremonial
> Kiss,
> mi myth and history, my
> Baptism, my

Baby Jesus, Niño Manuelito, Cuzco Child of Maquey
your diapers drying on the grass.
Chained down in Ollantaytambo
because sometimes you escape

to visit your sister
and fall asleep on the bamba

Ama wayqey manchankichu
wayqechallay fulanito
never fear little brother
little unknown brother

Jesus at the festival when the llamas are sacrificed
your face smeared with their blood
when all the dead guerrilleros are brought out
each perfectly preserved, even
the eyelashes, mi

Jesus quoting Marx, his words
flying from your lips
at the center of your green cross
spouting leaves, banners woven
from your outstretched arms, k'irinchasqa Apu
Sach'ag rurun Churi, Wounded God
Son of the Seed of the Tree

Jesus, mi Sapa Inca, mi martyr Tupaq Amaru,
Jesus mi presidente, mi son of a virgin, mi
Combatir y Resistir

Cristo de Blanco, negra
sum se formosa, je Sus
lover of my soul all over this earth, almas
mias above
this town
Cuzco your halo of Sun
kiskapillu of thorns
inside and out, your people
brought forth
from your rainbow blouse, your
bleeding red finger
on your burning red heart

yo hatch katchkani
Manan
yo hatch katchkani

El Corazón, our universal
Orphanhood

the murdered boy
inside every living man

Jesus the female in the male denied
Jesus the Indian in the race denied
Jesus the boy sacrificed to the father
Jesus the girl sacrificed
to every living man

Jesus our most ancient prayer
save the children from their father
save the people from the State

      this murder of the son
      too close to his mother

      this dying for the Father
      to escape the Mother

      this martyrdom
      to prove manhood, to be above
      all men

      this death on the cross
      rather than life on Earth

      this worldwide religion
      of gender war
      this Christmas and Crucifixion

        the making of the child
        by the Mother

that it might be unmade
by the Father

this hatred of Earth, this hatred
of life, this hatred
of woman, this hatred
of man, mi

hija, mi

hijo, yo

mismo

this worldwide worship

of Death

 Outside the cathedral
 an old woman
 load on her back
 pockets full of coca leaves
 prays to the god
 in the window

 whose gold and silver head
 is resplendent with amethysts
 pendants shimmering the light
 of heaven

 though it is to the black circles
 beneath his eyes
 it is to the boy
 murdered enemy of his father
 rotting inside

she brings
her white lilies

Airampu unullan kayqa
nillanki mare
confites hank'allan kayqa
nillanki mare

and say that the blood
is but crimson water
and that the rain of stones
is but a handful of sweets

7. Parthenon Virgin in Stone

a. Mama

Queen of the Cuzco Virgins
is the Virgin of Bethlehem.
She is the Conquering Virgin
the miracle worked by the Mamachas.
She is
the Mamacha.

b. Outside

In the first five days of the Conquest
the Spanish mass-raped the Chosen Women
at the mountain village of Caxas

five hundred Virgins of the Sun
forced out
into the plaza

the Inkas kept off
by crossbowmen
until the soldiers
were worn and spent. Then
they went off to continue
the Conquest.

c. Inside

There were many houses of Chosen Women
throughout the Empire. But none
like the House of Cuzco
guarded as sacred.
The Wives of the Sun
lived in perpetual retirement
in perpetual virginity

Punishment for profaning the Aqllawasi
was terrible, the virgin
buried alive, her lover
hanged, his family,
all his relations, friends and neighbors
killed, his village emptied
as an evil place

In 1601, after the Aqllas
wedded to and abused by
the Spanish Conquerors
had died, the nuns
of St. Catherine took refuge
in the great house
and again young women
grew old in the convent.
From the moment they entered
the world ceased to exist.
They devoted themselves
to God alone.
When they died
they were buried in the vaults
with the Aqllas.

d. Yma Sumac Present

But inside
Kusi Qoyllur, Joyful Star
a secret daughter

Kusi's father
the stern Inka Pachakuteq
would not forgive her
for letting her eyes
fall on a man
of the people

Ollanta

general of the Antis
triumphant in a hundred battles
conqueror of a hundred pueblos

> *"but he had not risen so high*
> *as to aspire to the hand*
> *of a Daughter of the Sun"*

Kusi was imprisoned
in the House of the Virgins of the Sun
for ten years. There
in the first year, unknown to anyone,
for no one entered the inner rooms
she gave birth to a daughter

  Yma Sumac

e. In a Land Where Virgins Are Named Mama

Outside the Palace of the Serpents
we stand before the convent,
The Virgins of the Sun.
My girl, mi Mama Shawn, mi ñusta, mi
nacida inocente asks

"What is a virgin, Mom?"

Inside I am walking
a thousand years up my continents
see
not a soul

In this legendary land
there are no las jóvenas.
All the thirteen-year-old girls

are mothers. Inside I know
my daughter is not a virgin
the way men mean
yet so virginal,
the way I raised her,
Mendocino, she's never known
the word.

She's knowledgeable about sex
but innocent of the sexes
the way I raised her
wanting her to love
her fathers.

I touch the smooth white squares,
Neruda's *stone within stone*
hear the girls
buried alive in the foundations
their screams at sixteen
against culture's
scale of beauty

the most beautiful
sacrificed to the sun

the second most beautiful
imprisoned as nuns
never to see
the sun

third most beautiful awarded as concubines,
weavers of the clothes, elaborate flags
under which the armies
march

as if beauty
is not in the eyes of the beholder

as if one man's beauty
must be God's decree
all must see
as he sees

I touch the white stone
hear the people sob, *Mama-cuna!*
your daughter *most beautiful.*
I watch her father tortured and killed
to hide her. *Inca!*

your stoned passion for walls!

the worship of the inhuman in all civilizations!

all our daughters born in the convents of cultures!

the flight of all children from time immemorial
from the First God

the flesh and blood from which we come
Mama
first Virgin
Unknowable. Unconquerable
female body, maker
of our death as well as our life, why
we hate her, why
we hate
nature.

I think to tell her
a virgin may have many lovers
but like the moon
she can never be possessed.

I think of Qori Oqllo, sister-wife to Manko II
who martyred herself in this square
rather than accept the hand of a Spaniard.

I think of the men who protested in her behalf
who died therefore terrible deaths
one of them being
Yma Sumac's grandfather.

o, she is inside her grandfather
inside the convent
freeing her mother, freeing
her father, her brother

little goddess little true
Self

Nevertheless, it is time, I know,
to tell my daughter,
my sixteen year old
the meaning of men.

"A virgin," I say the words carefully,
"is one who has not had
sexual intercourse."

But here at culture's altar
where She
is buried alive,
here where she is forever veiled from the world
that dies for need of Her,
here, where all the past uses of that word
virgin
fall in on her like stone
though I defined it without judgment or anger
my daughter, O virgin undone,
understands

"Are there any good men, Mom?"

8. South America Mi Hija

We Peruvians live in the hope that Inkari will put on his head, his torn arms and legs and lead us to liberty. That is a legend. But Inkari is Tupaq Amaru and thus the legend is but the signal for the appointed day. From the deepest graves and the most oppressive prisons, from the most subdued people and the most obstinately shackled consciousness, flow legends to make death musical, misery poetic, the darkness of conscience light, forgetfulness loving and loneliness companionable.

a. The Shining Path

Walls within walls Friday night when I walk
into Simon Bolivar's University of Cuzco,
unknown tongues blaring from the speakers
all this first day into the Square of Weeping
when my daughter and I arrive, Marxism, Leninism, Mao Tse Tung,
Sendero Luminoso, Tupaq Amaru.

Stunned, I sit down on the Inca's ancient wall
beneath the porticos that claim it Spanish
though the moon tells me the stones are alive
and weep. *I have been here before.*
A political convention in French Quebec.
A dream of flight from Vietnam
and a cruel European love
to the California northcoast.

Then I see on my right a great hall of the people assembled
thousands in their native costumes
beneath the great banner that declares
Quechua and Aymara
the first languages of Perú

and I understand as I understand Quechua and Aymara
these people

in the stadium that rises all sides to the ceiling
from the four suyus of the land divided as the seasons
wearing their colors from the planets and stars
their terrible symbols as if from revelations
mask upon mask, flag beyond flag

who rise from their seats roaring *Compadrazgo!*
in whose throats the love and the hate, *tierra o muerte!*
the cries they may die
the knowledge they may have to, the belief
the only way
the path that shines

and I understand as I understand myself
America

b. *Compadrazgo Means Spiritual Link Between Two People*

In the spring of 1979, Edith Lagos, 15, led a massive high school student strike in Ayacucho, the first action of Sendero Luminoso. In September 1982, at 19, she was found murdered, cut up by the bayonets of the military police. Despite intimidation and the danger, 30,000 people attended her funeral, almost half the city's population.

Inside a young woman
so near I still

can touch her, raised
on two stone tiers, wearing
blue jeans, old boots, a fitted
blue velvet jacket

beneath long black
hair. *Inca,* but not
the native costume
of woman. I can

touch her still, she carries on
beneath my stare
as if I'm not here,
lobbying for her right to speak, her
protest. This could be
Berkeley. Boston. It's
Cuzco, female
soul so fierce, intelligent, so
alone, Yma Sumac crying
five octaves around the world
the love and the hate, the strongest
wind, Amerrique. She is
any radical girl, so many I have known,
myself, one of three women
in the thousands of men
I watch, having walked
stunned in the high altitude
into the real Perú

beautiful men in their pointed knitted hats
with earflaps, red and pink,
their banners and staffs, turquoise and gold,
their purple ponchos, leather sandals, wildest weavings
lobbying for position, their turn
to protest
to cry

comrade! compañero! compadre! compadrazgo!

I keep pondering from what do these people rise?
With what knowledge are they armed?
How do the legends, the music, the poetry, the clothes,
the consciousness
continue to flow, and this girl, Edith
Lagos, mi
hija, mi

virgin

she who belongs to no man's tribe
whose roots she had to cut, more
binding than any man's, more
cutting, more

radical, more
painful

> *Inside the woman*
> *all the people*

in whose throat DESENCÁDENAR LA FURIA
DE LA MUJER
now the birds, the cuy, the winds
bring the whole hemisphere, Edith Lagos
from the deepest grave, the most
oppressive prison

so near I can touch you still
outside of time, your cheek
of geography, your velvety shoulder, your breasts,
your photo in all my country's papers
where you carry on, *tierra o muerte!* your name
means

battle and *lake,* your blue velvet
over your blue jeans

will be said, will be
sacred, we vow it, Goddess, we
vote it

you are the only revolution
the only future, mi

compadrazga, sweet
girl

Edith!
Get up!

Put on your head
your torn arms and legs, lead us

c. Edith Lagos Present

Who were the boys
who killed the girl,
Edith Lagos?

Sons, all sons,
mine and yours.

Why did they kill her?
How, in the great boy of the heart?
In the great yearning halfness of his loins?
At home with his sisters?
In love with the girl?
In the worship of his mother?
In the service of his country?
In the love of freedom?

   Fear of the First God
   Female
   From which he comes

   Grief for his First Love
   he has to leave

   Need for the body
   to labor
   he goes to battle

Jealousy
of the one who makes life
so he kills

Hatred of the Indian
inside himself
Hatred of nature
inside the woman
Fear of eros
inside outside the world
Fear of death
so he kills

Maleness he seeks
so weak
in the culture
he murders

nature outside him

his mother
inside him

9. Mamapacha the Loving Mother of Men

Inside the crooked window, the thick adobe walls,
the earth quakes and the people float
on the mythic view. Inside
I try to hold the people, carry them back
in this Panama hat I bought for you
from the market at Cuzco.
Watch out, the Indian warned me, *for those men with knives.*
I looked to where she pointed.
The men sat on the convent steps,
watched me.

Out the window the earth shudders again
in the long afternoon. In Colombia
two hundred die. In Bolivia
a government changes hands.
In my country you betray me.
The people cry, parade in the Square of Weeping
their black Jesus, Lord of the Earthquakes.
The musicians blow the legbones of their dead,
strum the armadillo's shell, the poet sings
porque mi patria es hermosa.

> *Inside I am carried in dream by you*
> *and the first man I loved, my daughter's father,*
> *to the attic of the community house.*
> *In the highest place, which is like an ovum,*
> *you lay me on the bed, attend me*
> *like altar boys*
>
> *like workers at some ancient stone*
> *like doctors at an abortion*
> *like government at the people*
> *like boy soldiers in flight of their mothers*

Inside my body is a body
and blood pouring out my vagina
a hemorrhaging we can't stop
the blood of a lost civilization, a flood
like gods, like Indians, like Conquistadors, like priests,
blood of all the virgins and all the sons born
from inside woman

    We get our dead child out,
    then off the bed, stinking
    hunk of meat, stillborn
    humanity. Ruin

        Outside the blood flooding everything, drowning
        the hungry, washing the walls
        so technical
        eros can't move
        between them.

VII. The Heights of Macchu Picchu

The Homeric Hymn tells us that Demeter's supreme gift to humanity in her rejoicing at Kore's return was not the return of vegetation but the founding of the sacred ceremonies at Eleusis, considered a key to spiritual survival.
                                                —Adrienne Rich

Eleusis ... means "arrival." It was said of initiates that they had arrived. Central to the Mysteries celebrated at Eleusis is the re-enactment of the mother's losing and finding her daughter, Persephone, the Primordial Maiden, called the Kore.
                                                —Nor Hall

There, in a great blaze of light, the queen of the dead, Persephone, appeared with her infant son, a sign to human beings that "birth in death is possible ... if they had faith in the Goddess." The real meaning of the Mysteries was this reintegration of death and birth, at a time when patriarchal splitting may have seemed about to sever them entirely.
                                                —Adrienne Rich

When the Spaniards arrived in Cuzco
the famous sacred fire
lit at each Inti Raymi
in June, the winter solstice,
and cared for by the aqllas,
was still burning in the Aqllawasi.
The noise of the conquest
had not penetrated the walls of the closed convent
when Hernando de Soto
rode in on his horse.

The conqueror's eyes lit on the lovely girl
Mama Killa
the guardian of the sacred flame.
Without hesitation
he picked her up in his arms
and galloped off with her
on the crupper of his horse.

The white man's sacrilege shocked the Indians
who managed to get back the dishonored wife of the Sun
to offer her life in atonement.
From the sacrificial altar
Mama Killa spoke to her people

> *"I die content*
> *because my eyes will never see*
> *the fall of the Empire*
> *of the Children of the Sun.*
> *The wings of death fill the sacred sky of Cuzco.*
> *In its streets will run the blood of its sons,*
> *and everywhere there will be grief. Sisters,*
> *I advise you to go far away*
> *beyond the white mountains*
> *for you too may fall*
> *into the brutal hands of the strangers*
> *who respect nothing . . ."*

Her words were endorsed
by the fall of the royal condor
which died in the great patio of the aqllas
after a mortal struggle with a hawk.

The priests interpreted its defeat
as a tragic omen
of the terrible days ahead
for Tawantinsuyu.

The virgins broke up in disorder
and it is thought
most of them took refuge
in Machupiqchu,
the secret city
concealed for centuries.

—Alfonsina Barrionuevo (translated and versified by author)

Sullen and taciturn, the man of the Andes fell back on himself and turned his eyes to his own world filled with stars and silence, clean as the crystal palaces of the mountains, eternal in the unknown dimension of stone, and went on believing in the shelter of his own things, in the warm protection of the earth that fed him with its juices. The mixture of blood was obvious. But if the father was white and imposed his authority, the law of might, the mother gave her heart to the child and with it her dreams, her way of thinking and feeling, her roots.

—Alfonsina Barrionuevo

What cloud is that cloud
Gathered so close?
Probably my mother's tears
turning to rain.

—from the Quechua

1. Valle Sagrado de la Inkas

Ahead out the window the local train
pulls us up the Urubamba River
past the cemeteries whitewashed
for the Day of the Dead,
past the silent stone fortresses
that guard the Sacred Valley of the Incas.
Saqsaywaman, Pisac, Ollantaytanpu, Huaman-marca,
Patallajta, Winay-Whayna, Botamarca, Loyamarca.
Inside, chatter of Quechua, bodies never bathed,
reek! chew coca leaf, bob a sea
of white stovepipe hats
over layered skirts, their bleeding reds,
their crying blues, their babies on their necks
chewing nipple.
An old man too old
hauls wet gunnysacks,
drips down the aisle, oozes down my arm
rotten bananas.

Inside a pale green bug crawls the window
looking for the outside.
Mi hija takes it so personally, jumps, *I hate that bug!*
Inside a man is getting up from his seat
and with his ticket to Macchu Picchu
is smashing the bug.
We are both stunned, this was not
her hatred. She sobs, *I thought
he was helping it out the window*

where now I can see the Virgins of the Sun
fleeing up the valley from the sacking of Cuzco.
We leave our ghost in a long snake of train smoke.

2. Alturas de Macchu Picchu

Then up the ladder of the earth I climbed
through the barbed jungle's thickets
until I reached you Macchu Picchu

a. *Sube conmigo, amor Americano*

Out the window a city
hidden like a condor's nest
high between the sacred peaks
Macchu Picchu and *Wayna Picchu*
the Old and the New
city from which the Incas plunged,
some believe, seventy years
to attack the Spanish
in Cuzco

and beneath Earth
the full moon
in my Taurus,
la luna llena
in the Scorpio moon of her Sun,
in this moment of our rising
in the International Year of the Child
two thousand feet straight up
this climbing
three thousand steps

> *a shepherd and his alpacas*
> *on the stone highway far below*

> this door
> to the jungle basin, *la ceja de la montaña*
> these headwaters
> of the Amazon

we climb, *Madre de piedra, espuma de los cóndores*

above the clouds
that splash below us like the sea
"Oh Mom!" she shouts back, "I want

to always travel!" The jóvenes follow
my blond llama, my funny vicuña.

What do I tell her of you, mi amor norteamericano?
What do I tell her of her father, the Russian
who fled her birth?
How do I tell her of men with women?
How do I not betray her brother?
How do I answer what I must
and not betray her?
There are

good men.

b.

Stone within stone, and man where was he?
Air within air, and man, where was he?
Time within time, and man, where was he?

Now we come to the end of the world,
up the last step, around the corner

to see you

Macchu Picchu

everlasting rose, our home

to be stunned
by your strangeness

the questions

pull from outside all stone, all air, all time, all flesh

Macchu Picchu

unpeopled city
intact
geometry, your quipus laid
in stone peaks

Macchu Picchu
your terraces, waterways, squares and temples,
your high gabled walls of interlocking homes,
your *bruised*
boulevards. Snowcapped
teeth! Gale
at a standstill on a slope.

Macchu Picchu

abstract composition two square miles

crystalline rectilinear immutable symmetries,
right angles, perpendiculars, horizontals,
diagonal staircases and trapezoidal doors,
gates and niches without a curve
except where the walls slant in
to withstand
earthquake

Macchu Picchu

hanging city
tallest crucible
single sculpture

single architectonic complex
abandoned for no known reason
at no known date

Macchu Picchu

a science fiction fantasy, una

epopeya

too high above the swirling Urubamba, *techo marino*
too sacred this sky forest, *dentadura nevada, piedra amenazante*
too geometric this door to the altiplano, *en la boca vacía*
too terrible this door to the jungle, *rascar la entraña, Amazon*!

> *Mother of stone, sperm of condor,*
> *who lived here?*
> *Stone of time, stone of flesh, why*
> *did they leave?*
> *Ruin of civilization, America*
> *what do I tell my daughter?*
>
> *What do I tell her, my sunny virgin, lost*
> *little girl from my body,*
> *of her country, the world she wants to find*
>
> *of its hatred for women, its story*
> *of genocide and the raped, the stoned, this place*
> *where human agony created*
> *a perfect, a stupendous, a beautiful*
> *ruin?* The Devil,
> *spit the old woman in Lima*
> *at her, mi hija*

must be beautiful.

c. *I ask you . . . show me . . . allow me . . . to . . . touch el hombre*

Echoes of wind
answer up the narrow canyons.
Thunder rolls through the sheer cut
we came through.
Lightning circles the needle peaks,
Macchu, Waynu.
Clouds float through the streets, engulf
my girl, Shawn Colleen, the jóvenes
who follow her.

Looking far down on a red helicopter.
Quiet. The quiet.
Mantur, the valley, bursts like a shattered mirror
a new world. Silence.

> *The graves found here
> are of women*

Yma Sumac, cry and scream! I walk
your streets. Macchu Picchu,
American city of Sappho, Isle of Lesbos,
headwaters of the largest river on earth
down which the Spanish explorer
Orellana floated four thousand miles
to the mouth on the equator
in pursuit of the rumors, the legend

away
from the source, this
nation
of female warriors

I walk through your temples Macchu Picchu
ruin of perfect ruin

aloft with so much death, a wall, with so much life
and pray

       Stone within stone, and woman, *where was she?*
       Air within air, and woman, *where was she?*
       Time within time, and woman, *where was she?*

When the furious condor batters my temples
(allow my hand to slide down a hypotenuse
of milk bodice and moon blood!)
I too like the poet
see the ancient being, the slave, the sleeping one
in the fields, I see a body, a thousand bodies, a woman, a thousand
men under the black squall, black with rain and night,
stoned with the leaden weight of statuary:

       Mama Wako, daughter of Viraqocha
       Mama Oqllo, heir of the green star
       Mama Rawa, granddaughter of the turquoise
       Mama, O Mama Mama Mama

                  rise up
                  to birth with me

                  my daughter

3. The Virgin: She Who Is Unto Herself

Inside a high round room
we learn the sacrifice
of the virgins was here.
"Oh, honey," I say, as we boost ourselves up
onto the stone altar, sit
shoulder to shoulder
"all women are virgins
because we have not yet
been loved."

The watch slips then
from her long deer limb
shatters on the altar
of the Virgins of the Sun

and she laughs

and the wind whistles her laughter
down the three thousand steps
blows her laughter around the llamas
fucking in the square
roars her laughter through the narrow canyon
of the divine Urubamba
over the Vilcambamba Cordillera spine
lifts the condor over the shepherd of alpacas
a mile below on the stone highway
that leads into the jungle

Then echoes of my girl like ocean waves
like dead lips congregating to tell me
splash with thunder, knives of lightning
back up the sheer cut, back over
the Lost City

and I hear
in her laugh at broken time
your sacred vows to me

    as I climb back up the continents
    as I step from the bus to California
    as I walk down the dark road to the sea
    to find you on the night porch of the inn
    as the poet hurries by in the dark and snickers
    the bond of your brotherhood
    and you tell me
    you will be free
    of us

The shudder goes through me

    alone above the earth
    amazon beneath the earth

    South America mi Eurydice
    South America mi hija

as the song of your brotherhood
the instruments of your gender
pours through the hemispheres

an evil struck, caressed, plucked and bowed
across the genitals of Earth
to serenade the Devil, beautiful
Brother

and leave us
horas, días, años,
edades ciegas, siglos estelares
unknown worlds, star
wars, Augusto Pinochet, Monroe
Doctrine

down under all
betrayed America

Pluto! Orpheus!
     a good man, husband
     the one I love most   Son
     father of my children, mi
     amor
          (to find you
          I have brought her this far

as the earth is a virgin   unknown   unloved   unexplored
unmated   untouched

I touch the stone
     (the terrible struggle through stone to remember
and know

     Inside this body is a woman

     inside of which is a word

     which has never been read

     which is a daughter

     and a son

     inside of which

     God dwells

     who is a Virgin

     who is a Couple

     who is Love

I touch the stone
and know you
Esposo!
a good man

your need to silence
Eros

      you will betray me
      you always have
      Son of woman
            (you said the fear of the mother
            is the hatred of woman
            is the hatred of nature
      Son of mine
            is the fear of death
      you will betray her

      you always will

I touch the stone and see
Inkara and Collura
Isis and Osiris
Adam and Eve

the two million year chemical
the apple that put the couple to sleep

fruit of knowledge, fruit of
good and evil, fruit of
gender

I shout the words
to the far north
I love you (I always will)
Blow the kiss

good-bye

give you back, Oh Orpheus
　　　　　　　　　　(who in greed and lust
　　　　　　　　　　looked back, objectified
　　　　　　　　　　her)
oh North America
waiting for us among your violins
your weapon
el confuso esplendor, la noche de

gender

war

of the
sexes

and sit here

　　　　Apegadme los cuerpos como imanes

your daughter

before you　　　behind you　　　above you　　　beneath you

　　　　más ancho que el mar y que sus islas

your mother

　　　　Hablad por mis palabras y mi sangre

in the genital city

Amazon city

of the old and unremembered
human heart

my hand plunged
to her womb
held all this time, *horas, días, años,*
edades ciegas, siglos estelares
by the jungle, mi yunga
that overthrew him

      that overgrew the Garden
      as in the dream of evolution
      as the child from the parent
      as the parent from the grandparent
      as the continent adrift
      from the continents

as your bow searches the strings
for the tune it will play

life or death

on this planet

4. Ceres and Kore on the Seat of the Sun

And on this dial the condor's shadow

a. Sun Goddess

Ten minutes to noon.
We sit on Intihuantana.
Where the Sun Is Tied.
A one inch shadow.
Thunder

    I love you Shawn Colleen
    mi Inti Chinan, mi handmaiden
    of the Sun

Thunder rolls through the canyon beneath us

    "The Seneca saw the sun
    as the head of the murdered goddess.
    The Cherokee saw her
    at dusk and dawn
    as the Menstruating God.

    The Incas said the sun
    sometimes marks the moon
    with menstrual blood.
    Those dark streaks
    across its face.

    The United States and the Soviet Union say
    they will expel the sun

    Now nuclear war
    will bring arctic darkness.
    The sun will be blocked
    by oceans of soot.
    Ice will finish
    what the firestorms start.

The heavens will grow dark
as in that empty time
before creation
because man thefted
by political fiat
the sun's secret."

"In a nuclear war, Mom," she consoles
"South America will survive.

Who would bomb
Perú?"

b. Noon

When there is no shadow
the call comes
to return to the train
In that instant
eight Brazilians
gather beneath us

take our picture

then run back down

We run up the condor's wings

Hide in her feathers

5. Photograph of the Virgins on the Sun

as the daughter is the core of the mother

As the present is a woman in orgasm
Psyche's coffin of divine beauty
has been dropped. *Llikichiri.* Sunwind.
We are blind in her rays. *Mamacuna.*
We are awake.

Sunlapse. Sunloved. Sacrificed
to the sun. Too much
time. Nuclear wash
of the world. Omphallos.
We are color of the llamas
fucking behind us. Color of her stones
Macchu Picchu. Positive
sun ions. Negative
thundering falls ions.
Color of chica, drunk
Amazons.

> *Daughter*
> *Deepest loneliest hole in the universe*
> *Most familiar, most unknown, most betrayed*
> *Aphrodite from her father's severed genital, root of Africa*
> *Achankarey most beautiful Virgin who grew the Koka Akulli*
> *Girl. The soul of all lost selves*
> *Vagina. Where the goddess is lost*
> *Where the hearts of murdered virgins are buried*
> *The hearts of all genocide victims*
> *Your body of light, body of myself*
> *Mi Inti Raymi, mi Parthenon, mi Sendera Luminosa*
> *Most beautiful sacrificed to the sun*
> *My love poem to the continents, my*
> *Machupiqchu*

All the lost languages, my two million year hymn
falling through the hole of eternity

Huaca
Vagina

I see our two faces, the One
we've never found, the Goddess
Mute, the past
coming at us from the future

Dark of the moon, as night as I am day
Manko and Raymi
You are male
I am female
Sun on sun

you are silver. Coya. Virgin. Muse. Nuera. Mi Yunga. Menstrual
blood. My southern
oscillation.
I am the Goddess. Hag of all mystery.
North American hegemony. Mother
broke asunder by the quakes.
Whore.

You. My Queen of Hades, Persephone, bringer
of destruction. My
mirror. The door
to Hell. And outer space. My
Blue Indigo
new soul
aura never known on Earth before
one of the first, a scout
for the Indigos
birthing now
to save us. Your face
still growing, gold sprouts

curling straight up. My face
growing down like a root, releasing
my crown of leaves to Heaven.

Ruin of ruin, my hand in your vagina.
Your body came out of mine.
Our mouths are identical twins.
Labia minora, labia majora.
Yours is about to speak,
mine demurely shuts.
Blonde on blonde, our hair
the same cut, identical line
of zygomatic arch, opal
neck. Your skull
out of mine, mine
out of my father's, his
from his mother's,
Lura Maude.

You have penciled the brows over your father's eyes
which look directly into us
the future, eight
Brazilians.
Red of your left eye, red of my ovary, so green, so
burning, his stare from the East, Mars, prostate
delivered. Hija, who'd dare
take your Scorpion sting?
Though the lonely hollows
already know betrayal, a small town
on the map of Russia.
The illness of your second year
pocks the left temple, lunar
evidence of my guilt. Darien,
five continental plates
grinding into each other.

My eyes show no mark of the writer.
The tattoo, the lead of pencil
I jabbed at three into my right cheek
doesn't photograph. My eyes
look down and away, seeking
your shadow, *la ceja de la Amazona*.
Beneath the left eye, two lines
already Inca, trapezoidal,
and the dipper. Always
the eye that embarrassed me, red
of my other ovary, eye
of the 6th House, small
eye of the Virgin, the Witch's
Eye, smaller
eye of Mercury, which, yes, after all,
premonitory star, is
the Blind Eye
of the poet

> *and eye of my mother, side*
> *that looks like her*

> *when I was your age*
> *I first saw her*
> *in the mirror*
> *I rearranged my hair*
> *and there she was*

> Yes!

> *she cried*

> side of your face

> that isn't beautiful

> *I felt so bad once again*
> *for my mother and myself*

221

Her side, my side, your side girl
the unloved side

that knows too much

her Eye

I've always tried to hide

from the lover out of kindness
from the lover out of need

a sweep of hair, rape of lock

over her Eye, oh

you
her tears falling

Grief of heart is proof of love.
Of good. This being
who you are.
I was a mirror in the noon sun.
When she looked at me
my mother went blind.
When he denied me
closing his doors, erasing his footprints
I came by other ways
all the unmarked roads, *Camino Inca*
so visible in your body.
When I got him inside me
my blood undammed.
He drowned his soul there.
Female. Big as Russia.
Niña. You.
My labor
to bring the two sides, day and night
together.

But ever since
¿donde esta la desaparacida?
I have been the Rose of Sharon
wandering the world in search of him, fear's
fragmented nations.
The ancient Hebrew at my throat
is the Linga Sharira, the Line of God
strung with birds of abalone
to ward off sorrow. Mi
Exodus.

We sit up here on Earth's core
Demeter's Laughless Rock
the seed sprouting in the terraced wall
behind our heads
two miles above the sea
in the November that is spring
our faces, sunrays, sunworshipped verses
planted in corn, food
of the Ancients, blue cob of seed
golden ear, golden rod
that founded Cuzco

while the snake rivers of your hair, divine Urubamba
flood my shoulders, hatuncocha where you wade,
como un río de rayos amarillos
como un río de tigres enterrados
leaping fish,
copper turning blue, night
turning the planet around to day, foetus
turning over in the minora
and majora lips of the boat, Charon
rearranging us
as he rows
the Line to God

the shining path strung with the moon and the sun
and all the lost breasts
of the Amazons

daughter of Manko and Raymi, Cartagena, daughter of Chernoble
all of China, the Cherokee, my
mother's sister Mozelle feminine of Moses
inside you

all my mother's nations Eva Perón
all my father's names Eden   Doubiago

west on the wind, mi Yma Sumac, my songbird
east around the earth, humanity's mass

north and south mi Senderista, my
Edith Lagos every hemisphere my
Eve

you come

Isthmus of Darien

Central to America

6. Lysistrata Amerrique

a. *Kore Would Appear Like Jesus to Men*

Now to tread the dance
Now to tread the light

Down the steps we fly
along the boulevards we run
Now we are a whirl, a leap, a ceremony
through the empty streets
beneath the condor
who soars

O Macchu Picchu, city of women
door from the jungle
door from outer space

> *what is the form*
> *of your soul*
> *flung open*
> *to the Invisible Ones*
> *everywhere*
> *in the universe?*

Now around the llamas fucking
now we laugh, now we search

bird wing
bird being

for the Mysteries
Eleusis of America
Now. This planet Earth
Now this seed   Mama
O Mama   Mama   Mama

In the beginning *Collura*
our middle names combined
Shawn Colleen and Sharon Lura
Colleen my mother's daughter, my sister *Donna Colleen*
Lura Maude my father's mother
Lura is unknown but *Maude*
is *mighty in battle* and
Magdalene

Now our girl, our woman, our future, our past
Now our daughter, our sister, our mother
Now our Isis, our Yma Sumac so beautiful
our sunset Osiris his penis gone down
Now we laugh now it's lost now we search
Now la luna llena in our Venus our full moon rising Mamakilla
Now Mama Mama Mama run with us, show us
proof of your passing

> *Here I was born, my mother's house, memorize*
> *the first place.*
> *Here our observatory, where I learned*
> *the planets and stars, remember*
> *time and death.*
> *Here I knelt, say again*
> *the first prayer.*
> *Here I ran, here I ate, here I slept, redream*
> *the first nightmare.*
> *Here I bathed, oh beautiful body, here I birthed, never*
> *forget*

> *on this terrace, in this room, in this meadow*
> *on this step, in this hall, on this square*
> *beneath this roof, this rock, this peak, this*
> *grass*

> *I was kissed, pututu, pinkuyllu, quena, antara,*
> *charango, blood of my womb, yaravi*
> *Here in the Three Windows of God, Tanpu T'oqo,*

purified, looking east,
I waited. There

up that terraced peak
is how he climbed.
Here is where he found me, here

we fell together

On this stone he said I love you.
In this temple he first placed
into my hands his penis
O holy rod that founded Cuzco

Here in this field he placed it
inside me
holy

Huaca

b. Amazon

who wanders grinding frozen syllables
black languages   she comes

with clouds, comes quickly to my veins and my mouth.
She leads us through the streets, her feet
like fine brass, her eyes
like flame of fire, her soul
sick with love

> "*In the beginning God was a couple.*
> *Inkari, a man   Collura, a woman.*
> *Then the Fall.*
> *God became a man, the men*
> *we birthed. And Creation*
> *a war.*

We waited, having faith, in love with our men,
their children we birthed.
Each time we believed
in our *children*
God had returned.

We loved.
Generation within generation, war
within war, screams within prayers,
his child in my womb, armies
in our labor we waited.
Each love
a new beginning, each birth
a new belief, a new Messiah, a new
Empire

daughter from mother from grandmother
mother into daughter into granddaughter
son from mother into granddaughter
into great grandson, we waited

generations within civilizations into new races,
our men into cannon fodder, our fathers
into our brothers into our lovers
our husbands making fodder
of their sons, fidelity

into tragedy into absurdity, Penelope
for Ulysses, Kusi Collura
for Ollanta, Son of my Love of my body

into my grandson, *eons*
we waited

for men in their worldmaking
to save us in our racemaking

for men
to make peace! How much

war, how much

flesh, how much suffering, how much hate,
how much history, how much heartbreak,
how much labor, how much

love

how many religions, how many saviors, how many
nations, how many worlds in ruins, how many
lovers, how many

men

we labored to bring forth
how many men

we held
when they returned

how much they needed, we thought
our femininity, how much we needed
their masculinity, to be part
of their world, how much

strength we gave them as men, how much strength
they gave us as women

but none, though we believed, though we loved,
were made closer
to God

a couple

each woman a new goddess
from which each man
launched

a new war"

c. God Is a Couple

"Who could put in words
the drama of the revelation
in each woman,
the courage it took?

Who could put in words
the immensity of the need for deliverance,
the extent of our grief, our rage,
the immensity of the decision
to live without men
for the rest of our lives?

Who could put in words
the drama of the revelation
in each woman

the courage to face
their narrow intelligence?
their reactionary psychology?
their emotional retardation?

Broken fragment of unfinished man!
Even your great poet
who came here before you,
poet of the slave, of the one asleep,

who cries, who prays
who invokes the Muse
stone of stone, age of the ages,

to pierce the walls
life of stone after so many deaths!

prays to see
not *humanity*—God
is a couple! *prays
to see*

men, high and low
*serviced
by women*

Juan Splitstones! Juan Coldbelly! Juan Barefoot! *How
could Neruda of such empathy? How
with the world on the brink?*

*How the historians ponder
the lost civilizations*

how our own men,

      my father

                my brother

                        my husband

                                my son

Why

*did we fuck
conquistadors?*

*You can feel me, poet,
when you touch the stone*

she is, he is, we are
the extinct condor
whose form is this city, one sculpture,
who soars now its empty streets
whose soul has been crushed

how the world ends
in the coffin
of gender."

7. Macchu Picchu: Women-Raised Children Will Always Produce the Patriarchy

a. *Who Could Put in Words*

Is it only at the end of the world
that we can pull back the veil?

Is it only on this brink
that we can make
the evolutionary leap?

> *The male is not to blame.*
> *Nor is the female.*
> *But the war*
> *is gender.*

> *The war*
> *is nuclear.*

b. Set, the Principle of Evil

Old woman in Lima,
my daughter
is not the Devil.

Nor are you. Nor am I.
Nor are your children,
your country, your race.
Nor mine.

Nor your God. Nor mine.

Nor is the Devil
the men
who murdered you,
raped her, pillaged

our sacred towns, castrated
our sons, destroyed
all civilization.

Nor is the Devil
male.
Nor is the Devil
female.

I touch the stone and know
the Devil

c. Gender

I touch the stone
where human agony created
a perfect, a stupendous, a beautiful
ruin, and know

a city of women
built by men

I touch the stone and know, male-identified Amazon
your city not different
than mens'

> *this stone designed to hold a person's head and hands*
> *in the sun*
> *for slow strangulation*

> *this stone on which*
> *the virgins were sacrificed*

Inca! Stupid Hombre! Viejo! Deceived
Amazon

his song
of history, his geometry, his rock work, his
barbaric conquests, his
society

his betrayal of the child,
the ego's rebellion, male *and* female,
from the mother

    how the world ends

    in the coffin of gender

            The child will descend
            these heights
            will descend
            the Great Mother

            in search of its father

8. Electra Amerrique

Up here men's feet found rest at night
near eagles' talons in the high
meat-stuffed eyries. And in the dawn
with thunder steps they trod the thinning mists
touching the earth and stones that they might recognize
that touch come night, come death.

a. *My Soul Turns to Stone*

The full moon rises with Electra, *the Lost Pleaid*
who disappeared just before the Trojan War
that she might be saved
the mortification of seeing the ruin
of her beloved city.

Noche elevada en dedos y raíces.
We lay our bags in the highest house,
the grass roof disappeared eons ago
with flesh. When Electra
shows herself to Earth
she does so in the guise
of a comet.

We lie here, side by side, stare
into the universe, the stars
like the stars on her father's wedding band.
Now the Scorpion with the sun has fled.
Now my moon, the Bull, hard and cold on us.
She says "I can hear the women who live here
whispering to one another.
I can hear them dancing, their cries
of love. Can you?"
Oh moon girl, Ishtar
outside of time they wander
Qollana, Payan, Kayo
on the rivering waters of

the hithering and thithering waters of
our menses, our mania
inside.
Now westward, forward, they blow
their breath across our bodies.
Cabellera del frío, acción del aire.
Now eastward, backward, *piedra amenazante*
in our eyes our hemisphere
watching.

> *Amor, amor, hasta la noche abrupta*
> *desde el sonoro pedernal andino*
> *hacia la aurora de rodillas rojas*

I tell her then of the other Electra
sister of Iphigenia who slew
her mother.

b. My Mother Couldn't Speak I Can't

I was a mirror in the noon sun
When she looked at me
my mother went blind

She was a mirror in the noon sun
When I looked at her
I went blind

To protect my mother
I didn't see her

To protect my mother
I didn't see
myself

To protect my mother and myself
I sacrifice you, my daughter
again and again

To protect
all that is holy
from my mother
through me
to you

to protect the virgin
the lost little girl
from the man
who can't love us
I go blank
as my mother went blank

> All my mother could do
> was go blank

> All I can do
> is go blank

> and pass the blank
> to you

c. *Will the Stones Speak?*

Everyone blames the mother
and all mothers blame themselves

Isis was condemned to pregnancy
by Set, *the principle of Evil,*
to never give birth
to never find the genitals
he tore from his brother, Osiris.

All my life. All your life
I have labored
to birth the words.
I have searched
for the male.
lost brother. lost father. lost son. lost lover.

If she birthed, if she found him
civilization (as we know it) would fall.
We would understand
gender.

All creation myths
are about God the Couple

All myths of the Fall
are of the loss
we fall into

Gender.

d. Clytemnestra Amerrique

Now in the terrible struggle to speak
I say again
what I've always said

Forgive him
He knows not
what he does.

> I was a child in my parents' home!
> My parents loved me!
> We didn't understand
> gender!

I feared your anger
female
would be the same as his
male.
War!
Why love
has always failed

I feared being thought
a manhater
so I denied
the evidence everywhere

my culture
hates women, hates
the feminine

       (hates you
       daughter

       but it seemed
       unfair, it seemed
       stupid
       to impose upon you

       manhatred

And I loved
the special place
I played in his life

he found in my arms
when he came home
from his worldmaking

he found in my bed
when he came home
from his wars

It is true
he needed me
It is true

I was the woman
behind the man
I was the woman
behind his wars

    All your life
    I rushed to tell you
    All my life
    my mother
    taught me

    Do not blame
    men

    Love the world

    Understand

    The male
    has no other role

Now I touch this stone
the world broken open
all the lost civilizations
embedded in you
Daughter
like precious stones

see my understanding
as martyrdom
as masochism to his sadism

see his martyrdom
as masochism
to his father's
sadism

    All my life I have fought
    the charge

    Masochism

    I knew

    Love

    But I didn't understand

    Gender

e. *My Soul in the Stone of a Woman*

I thought my love for you gave me wisdom, the key,
that with me, with my children
the world was changed.
My roots to all past mothers' cut
I thought we were beyond
gender.

I strove to be
simply the vessel
through which you were able
to come. Suffering his overbearance on the world
and on me
I was afraid of myself on the world
and on you,
your brother.
Always I feared
suffocating you.

Always I let you go
rather than cling to you.
I love you.
I raised you to question everything
I said to you.
I raised you in the spiritual discipline
to understand the Other
the other side, that everyone's truth
is the only truth.
(I didn't know
you would become the Other.)
I strove to preserve

you

the One I first knew.
Not a girl. Not a boy. Not me.

God.

Women have always known more than ego.
Than masochism.
They birth love
knowing only love can change the world.
But now I see I have always
just let you go.
I didn't understand the world.
My parents didn't understand gender.
I couldn't warn you.

Now I see my parents raped
believe
to be adult
is to be raped.
To be mature
is to rape.

Now I see
you have already suffered
the abuse I suffered.
Now you live in your fathers' stones.
Now I see like all mothers, time immemorial
I have handed you over

a virgin

to the patriarchy

f. Blank Like Nuclear War

Women go blank
in their wild desperation
for Amor

The soul goes blank
in its wild desperation
for love on Earth

Women go blank
for the next revolution
make daughters and sons
their political contribution

not seeing their children
descend into Hell

not seeing the man
blankest of all

    Blank is a wall
    centuries built

        I was pregnant with the world like a blank

Blanks the impotent make
in their munitions factories

      I passed the great blank

to fit
the universal holes
of the world's guns

to make the world
a blank

9. Iphigenia Amerrique

He is so close, the smell of granite
the glacier water of his eye
the insane stone of his flesh

the vein with his soul
about to explode
the left side of his face
impenetrable rock
so streaked with anger
so creased with age
so set with fear
so impotent with rage
so sexual Father

trying to speak

the unspeakable

his arm, his leg, his soul
flying out
unpredictable
lethal, out of
control

a good man
a great man
the man I love most

so evil
his State
all we have constructed
in the name of eros and civilization
personality
desire become habit become stone
so as not to know, not to ever
know

I move closer to him. I see
that he loves me. How much
I love him. Tell me,
Father, what
is wrong?

My terror that he will answer
is as great as his terror
he will speak
I know what he wants to say
What I cannot bear
to hear

the only knowledge
that can save us

my question
his answer

10. 72° West   13° South

Águila sideral, viña de bruma.
Bastión perdido, cimitarra ciega.
Centurón estrellado, pan solemne.
Escala torrencial, párpado inmenso.

a. Amerrique Forever

Awake. Far cry of the quena. Yaravi.
A lonely Amazon blowing the femur of her beloved.
Electra, my girl, amber rubbed to the shining one,
asleep.

Taurus full moon overhead. *Ola de plata*
in my eyes, *dirección del tiempo*
Toro de la luna, luz de piedra.
The South Node, all our karma, all our history
setting in the Fish
the Piscean Age descending.
And our Part of Fortune
right on the horizon, eight degrees Aquarius,
the house of marriage.

Túnica triangular, polen de piedra.
Lámpara de granito, pan de piedra.
Serpiente mineral, rosa de piedra.
Nave enterrada, manantial de piedra.
Caballo de la luna, luz de piedra.
Escuadra equinoccial, vapor de piedra.
Geometría final, libro de piedra.

I can feel
all the planets
in a fan-shaped trine
lined up beneath us
ready to rise

248

or rather
to greet us
as we fall back to them

first Mars, burning *la cuerda del cielo*
in Leo

then Jupiter
brightest god
conjunct all the future
the North Node of the Moon
shining from the head of the Virgin

then Saturn
at her groin, my poem, my girl, our Satan
the Devil now deep
in Earth's second house

then Pluto in Libra
Persephone's husband, ruler of the Underground
planet of death and transformation
now in the third, small and distant

an hour before the sun
now right at our core, our nadir, Pluto's
Kore, Persephone, the gaping hole he took her down,
root of all ancestors, the past.
Mother. Father.
Deepest part of the self, prostate, midnight
of the soul, daughter. Midnight
Sun.

Then Uranus, Revolution and Venus, Love
in the Scorpion's tail, the western side
of the Linga Sharira
origin of the universe
Mercury on the east, in the hooves
of Sagittarius

as we fall back to the east
back down and around to them
One thousand miles an hour
on our axis
around the sun 66,700 miles an hour
around the Milky Way in our solar system
605,000 miles an hour

to day and night, winter and summer
the foetus turning over

and over and over

> *Ventana de las nieblas, paloma endurecida.*
> *Planta nocturna, estatua de los truenos.*
> *Cordillera esencial, techo marino.*
> *Arquitectura de águilas perdidas.*
> *Cuerda del cielo, abeja de la altura.*
> *Nivel sangriento, estrella construída.*
> *Burbuja mineral, luna de cuarzo.*
> *Serpiente andina, frente de amaranto.*
> *Cúpula del silencio, patria pura.*
> *Novia del mar, árbol de catedrales.*
> *Ramo de sal, cerezo de alas negras.*
> *Dentadura nevada, trueno frío.*
> *Luna arañada, piedra amenazante.*
> *Cabellera del frío, acción del aire.*
> *Volcán de manos, catarata oscura.*
> *Ola de plata, dirección del tiempo.*

> my fear of my father's death
> my fear of my mother's death
> my fear of my children's death
> my fear of my death

b. *Sappho Amerrique*

I have a small
daughter, called
Cleis, who is

like a golden
flower

   I wouldn't
take all Croesus'
kingdom with love
thrown in, for her

11. Macchu Picchu, Why Did They Leave?

I'm rising
from the basin of the sea
in the sunlit architecture of my town
walking street after street
ingeniously terraced with our food
to the great house on the northwest bluff
of the United States.
From the East I see in clarity and oddness
structures of gold, circular staircases,
ballrooms and atriums, gardens
hanging from the infinite split levels
of the foreign country in the North, America
also. The last mountains, exile of the western gods,
fracture the clouds, as the sun in its rays
drops behind the highest, Mt. Olympus.
On the inland sea the Spanish believed
the passage to the Atlantic Ocean
a lone sail drifts
across the three plates of the world.

My townspeople are gathered on the highest level,
afloat in flowering pots and the clouds
of animal spirits. My old home
is a boarding house, rooms rundown, rented
cheap. I move around the western corner,
see the glass dome smashed, the rain
pouring in. In my geopsychic complex,
weather of time and heart, I wash
in the sea below, tidal sea
of grief, sea of concern, who
lives there now? Why
do they not love her?

Then to the highest terrace I'm rising.
Recline against the arched wall, the moon,
making me invisible, to see

you
entering from the bath
still dressing, your wet hair clinging
to your geometric, El Dorado face.
As if orchestrated, all of us, everything,
the ruin, the bluff, the Olympics, the Pacific, the two nations
present themselves
so deep is our feminine instinct to pretend
we don't see you moving now among us
telling your little jokes.
You look as you did the first time I saw you.
As if you had never seen me.

I rise to leave for the story
you want me to believe
for the pain I must not feel
for the woman you love in me

> *when the other woman enters*
> *the one from whom you have just risen*
> *who sings now until I have to know*
> *as everyone has always known*
> *your infidelities*

> > *(I need to get out of here*
> > *but I haven't the strength.*
> > *I can't stand up, I'm too ashamed*
> > *I can't stand to be seen, I've been hit*
> > *too hard. I can't leave.*
> > *I can't stand in my agony*
> > *to be away from you*
> > *the cause of my agony.*

In the castles of Spain
the Spanish didn't have
pools of water
until they encountered the Incas

who swam and bathed in every room.
I escape to your bath, stand now
above a deep pool of American thought,
hygiene and recreation, and consider
the wall

       a magnificent, irreplaceable work of ancient art
       the only record we have

or my life

       architecture, record and art
       of the time and place my parents loved

I'm broken so badly, I'm every creature
ever trapped in matter and thought, civilization
calcified as rock

as you play your violin at the door, virtuoso
your limpid and precious notes in harmony
with my weeping, el llanto
with the water turned on, with my going
under, wave upon wave, eons through time
in the baptism of suicide, our people's
religion

       when she appears at the door. Two of her.
       Reasonable. Beautiful.
       The innocent who kills me, my daughter, my sister,
       double my heartbreak, my vulva,
       dark of the Third World, shirtless,
       urging my sacrifice.
       And her other face, milk breast,
       familiar mother, Amazon, Aunt Mozelle,
       my mother's sister, sister of Moses
       besieging me

till I hatchet the great wall of art
leap across the crumbling stones
to Earth
my pack on my back, and flee
into the Unknown

Epilogue: The Dawn, Amor Amerrique

From my mother's sleep I fell into the State,
And I hunched in its belly till my wet fur froze.
Six miles from earth, loosed from its dream of life,
I woke to black flak and the nightmare fighters.
When I died they washed me out of the turret with a hose.
—Randall Jarrell

Mother
We are not of this world
a long time ago
it happened it was over:
the world the war the world war
I took you by the hand
through it
tiniest hand, tiniest star.
—Jack Hirschman

what is this mother-father
to tear at our entrails?

what is this unsatisfied duality
which you cannot satisfy?
. . .
[There is a] new Eve who comes
—H. D.

I come to speak through your dead mouths
—Pablo Neruda

What would happen if one woman told
the truth about her life? The world
would split open.
—Muriel Rukeyser

But the longer her hour is postponed, and therefore the more exhausted by man's irreligious improvidence the natural resources of the soil and sea become, the less merciful will her five-fold mask be, and the narrower the scope of action that she grants to whichever demi-god she chooses to take as her temporary consort in godhead.
—Robert Graves

1. *Psyche*

Psyche at Earth's core
doesn't know her mother betrayed her
(Earth is unknown
The soul knows only the search for love
(all over the earth
doesn't know
death
(Earth will explode

Consciousness is a created
creative event
a bucket full of water

It can be spilt
Consciousness knows death
but the Soul dives

into the deepest pool
comes up
only when Amor
loves her, loves Amor
only when she emerges
to the light

The Other is creating us
as we are creating it
We are not separate

but Psyche will hide
from even the self

Psyche is eternal

in her cocoon

on her butterfly wings

2. The Death Wish

I, Incan of the slime,
I touched the stone
and I said:

I touch the stone and see
every human being

raised by a woman

grow into a world
that hates
women

who grows then
to hate the self

humanity

I touch the stone
and see

our sickness

3. Mother

I touch the stone, the powerful proportion,
slide my hand down the perfect square
and know
terror
of the mother.

I touch my daughter, the powerful flesh
and know
God
and understand
the Fall
of all civilizations

I touch the stone and know
terror of flesh

terror of woman

terror of nature

terror of death

terror of Eros

terror of Soul

terror of the Unknown, Unnamed, Unsaved
inconsequential self

I touch the stone
and know
the rejection of the mother
is the origin of evil

Mother

who brings us to life
out of death
that we might return
to death

Mother

　　　her body is a vessel of death

Devouring hole. Abyss
inside forever
unconquerable

I touch the stone and know
male rule of the world
has its emotional roots
in female rule of early childhood

I touch the stone and know
the Son
his revenge against the mother
his pursuit of culture's authority
technology
as revenge
against nature, as revenge
against death

I touch the stone and know
the greatest love
The child's love for its mother

I touch the stone and know
the humiliation the child knows
so helpless
to its mother
so in love
with its mother

She who made her, fruit of her womb
She who fed him, milk of her breasts
She who cleansed her, milk of her breasts
She who taught him
  his body
  who taught him
  to speak
  who encouraged him
  to love
  who encouraged them
  to feel. She

in whose giant body they first were
in whose giant arms they first lay
in whose giant face they first gazed
She, first

God

I touch the stone and know the boy
who in having to find
male identity
must see *his mother*
In his first act of self
he must see his mother
female
must objectify her
woman
in order to see
all that she is
is all
he must not be

who in his going out
must reject her
must reject all that is woman
(will reject all of his women)
to become

a man

I touch the stone and see the girl
who in finding
female identity
turns only half away
from the mother
to the father
(never needs to objectify)
sees the woman is herself
she is rejecting
knows
self-betrayal, self-
hatred

who in her going out
to love the male
to be a woman
knows complicity
at the core of the self
with the patriarchy

       Mother who in the beginning for their father
       Mother who in the beginning for love
       Mother who in the beginning for their being
           She who opens
           inside
           that they may come
           outside
           She who knows in their going out
           they will hate her

       Mother who forever now in exile
       Mother forever now
       Eden lost

I touch the stone and know
the psychology
of gender

why women who raise the children
don't change the world

    as we could
    in one generation
    at any time, in any place in history

    in one generation!

    And why
    since we don't
    we are hated

I touch the stone and know
the hatred of woman
is the hatred of nature, why
we want to destroy
the earth.

I touch the stone and know
our fear of death
is our pursuit of death

I touch the stone and know
why the world is not
a more erotic place
why we don't fulfill
our sensual potential
why we are so afraid
of Eros
The rejection of the Mother (fear of death fear of flesh)
is the rejection of the erotic
the rejection of Love

I touch the stone and know
why we turn
again and again

from freedom
to the despot

The male, the father, second love
will always seem
freedom
from the first god, the first tyrant,
Mother

I touch the stone and know
the rejection of the mother
is the origin of war
The war between men and women
is the nuclear war
Children raised by women
always produce the patriarchy
The mother is always the one
we flee

for the father
second god, first act
of will

who therefore seems
freedom

of choice

who seems
rational authority, organized consciousness,
human mastery, manageable objective, distant ascetic, God
outside in the sky

not primitive, not blood, not flesh, not mortal, not mystery
not matter, not nature, not inside
but conscious leap
the mind, all the abstract considerations of language, abstract

thought, deliberation, enterprise, technology. Pater
spiritual salvation from mater,
the life-death cycle
on earth

I touch you, mi hija, and see
your absent father

that teenager, that sailor, that Russian
that boy
who lost both
(the boy always loses both)
his mother and his father

who lost us
in fear of love

who fled in fear of the feminine
in pursuit of the masculine

who fled us
to make war

who now seems to you
freedom

        (so attractive in his distance
        so far away in his heaven
        all the world you can travel)

O Daughter, mija, O
Son, mijo, I touch
the stone
and see

in the infant's turning from the mother
lies culture's turning from the feminine

in the child's turning from the parent
to find self identity

we turn from the mother, from the woman, from nature
we turn from life
to death
to war

to the Fathers

Daughter
in turning the son from us
they will turn
the sun from Earth

4. *Gender*

The male-female collaboration to keep history mad has become impossible to sustain.

a. Male

who comes to recognize himself as "Other."

He will know himself male
in the act
of rejecting
women (his mother

He will know himself
male
in the act
of objectifying
you
(his first act of self

He carries both
the male and the female
in his genital sacks

Is this why
he must
define himself?

He will know himself
male
when he doesn't
love you

when he is outside
disappearing
in search of his father
disappearing

when he finds himself
alone
on the battlefield
in killing, in death
in no, in
sadism, as
single
when he destroys
the earth

b. Female

You will know yourself female
in the act of love

You will know yourself
female
when you love
him

when he is inside
you

     (as you came
     from inside him

when you find yourself
lost
in his arms

as you knew yourself
undefined
in his arms

as you knew yourself
at one
in mine

It is semen that carries
the male and the female
What then is
female?
Is it without gender, or is it
both? You
who do not have to
define yourself

you who did not have to
see me, objectify, then
reject me
to find
gender identity

You who can float around
as the desired
in easy complicity
with the patriarchy

You
who will know yourself female
when you are the earth
(being destroyed)
Identity
with everything
(even your destruction)
Source
of all life. Source
of love, bloodbond
of pregnancy, even
death

And you will love him
when he comes home
from his worldmaking
from his fleshkilling

You will love him
more than your children
fruit of your body

You

for love of the male
to define yourself female
will hand over to him

your children

your son as soldier

your daughter as spoils

5. Father

a. Our Father Who Art in Heaven

I touch the stone and know
myself
turning from my mother
to my father

from inside whom
I came

now so distant, now so absent, father
now for whom I eternally long, now
my self always split

I touch the stone and know
the law of nature
When two particles intersect
then fly off
whatever happens to one
happens to the other

Father disappeared, father oh so distant
Father for whom I long, now my cells
always split, now the atom
split, now my century
death by cancer

I touch the stone and know
all selves
all cells
longing for the father

my mother longing for her father
my father longing for his father
my children longing for their father
their father longing for his father

all patriarchies
longing for the father

all religions
longing for the father

all nations
going to holy war
for God
the Father

Father for whom we flee the mother
Father on whose face we cannot look
Father who demands the sacrifice of the child
Father in whose body we are crucified
Father our disease, all of us
disappearing

I touch the stone
the father
from whom we come

who carries the girl's dress
the boy's tunic
to the genderless ovum

myself inside my father dying
my father inside of me returning
my son inside of me dying
myself inside my son returning

and know the man
in flight of his mother
(the core unit
the mother and child)
seeking purpose
seeking place

(seeking his father)
creates the patriarchy
enterprise and mastery
war and death

and know the woman
who also flees
the Great Mother
who also seeks
the distant father
from inside whom she came
from out of whom he comes
on whom she must depend
to survive the evil of his world
puts him first
before herself, before
their children

I touch the stone and know
the evolutionary step

b. The Phallocracy

I touch the stone and see
Isis
still searching
for the phallus

through the patriarchies
of all time all place
the male forever impotent
the male forever castrated
the male forever disappeared

and crucified he goes to be with the father
and crucified he goes to become the father
to resurrect

his missing part
his phantom member, his
disappeared
Father

to resurrect
his Father
as Death
the murdered boy
as Rape
the lost son

as bitterness and stink, our savior
from Mother

now his greatest
shame, the greatest
taboo

    his oldest

Adversary

6. *The Return of the Goddess*

a. *There Is a New Eve Who Comes*

I touch the stone and see
the Son
Kore holds in her arms

Her brother-lover-son

telling of a different
Male Female
Kore

I touch the stone and see
all men
as their mothers' sons

b. Love and the Evolution

Now as in the beginning of time
Uranus lies too heavily on Gaia
Earth begins to die
The children can't rise

Now as in the beginning of time
the mother urges her son
Time
to kill the father
too cruel   too powerful   too blind
Evil
in his sky

Now as in the beginning of Time
the son
knows the death
he must exact

must castrate
the patriarch, throw
the genital
into the sea

That Love may rise

7. *Hijo*

I touch the stone and know
the laws work only
if we stay afraid

self-ignorant, in
hubris

I touch the stone and see
the man touching the foam
resurrecting
as the Son
of man

I touch the stone and see
men returning to their mothers
their sisters
so our core relationship is not
the masculine imbalance
Father and Son

to restore the gender balance
of Nature, the Kore
of the Ancient Non-warring Times

Mother and Son

I touch the stone and see
the father
remembering
his physical bond
to the child

to all humanity
to Earth

knowing
to leave the child
is killing Earth

I touch the stone and see
the fathers returning to the children
so our ego turning from the parent
is not universally turning
from the woman
from all that is feminine
from nature, earth, life

I touch the stone and see
the fathers finding
the infants

when in the structure of personality
is formed
the structure of civilization

I touch the stone and know
children raised by men

I touch the stone and see
the world break open

8. *Hija*

I touch the stone
the world breaks open

Isis finds
her Beloved
in the foam of sex
her son threw

I touch the stone and see
the Son as Love

Jesus as his mother's son

Attis, Tammuz, Adonis, Osiris, Orpheus, Agamemnon, Oedipus
Inkari, Tupaq Amaru
Ayar Awka, the Golden Rod that founded Cuzco
Inti Raymi

Sequoia, Chief Joseph, Sitting Bull
Hinhamtuyalatkekat, Iyotaka
Crazy Horse

Whitman

Marx, Mao, Lenin, Sandino, Ché
Martin Luther King, Nelson Mandela
Neruda

my father, Cecil Frederick
my brother, Clarke Frederick
my son, Daniel Clarke

the son
not as child

but the son

        my husband your father our brother

as the true masculine, the son
as Time, evolutionary
savior, the sun the male
bonded to the mother

to the sister

to the daughter

to woman

to Earth

        mi hija

               Yo hatch katchkani
               Manan yo hatch katchkani
               Chaimita tapukui

1979–1989

Notes

I entitle my poem "South America Mi Hija" with deference. My meaning is *not* from traditional cultural imperialism, nor is it from traditional parental presumption or authoritarianism. My meaning is from the poet.

For this poem I am most indebted to Dorothy Dinnerstein, *The Mermaid and the Minotaur: Sexual Arrangements and Human Malaise* (New York: Harper & Row, 1976), the ground-breaking feminist interpretation and vision of Sigmund Freud's Oedipus complex theory, especially as he so bleakly develops it into the death wish theory (*Civilization and Its Discontents*), subsequently employed by Herbert Marcuse (*Eros and Civilization*) and Norman O. Brown (*Life Against Death: The Psychoanalytical Meaning of History*).

For knowledge and information of the Colombian, Ecuadorian, and Peruvian worlds, my sources have been many and varied. The most reliable and indispensable sources have been: *The South American Handbook* (Bath, Great Britain: Mendip Press, 1975, 1979, 1985), currently published in the United States by Prentice Hall Press, New York; Hiram Bingham, *Lost City of the Incas* (New York: Macmillan, 1963), and *Macchu Picchu: A Citadel of the Incas* (New York: Macmillan, 1970); Alfonsina Barrionuevo, *Cuzco, Magic City* (Lima: Editorial Universo S.A., 1969); Victor W. Von Hagen, *The Realm of the Incas* (New York: Mentor, 1957); Arnold and Harriet Greenberg, *South America on $15 a Day* (New York: Frommer/Pasmantier Pub. Corp., 1979).

Amerrique: (a-'mer-ē-kā). For further exploration of the origin of the name *America:* Jan Carew, "The Caribbean Writer and Exile, *Caliban,* 2, no. 2 (Fall-Winter 1978); Jonathan Cohen, "The Naming of America: Fragments We've Shored Against Ourselves," *The American Voice* 13 (Winter 1988); Zoë Anglesey, ed., *IXOK AMAR GO: Central American Women's Poetry for Peace* (Penobscot, Maine: Granite Press, 1987); *The Compact Edition of the Oxford Dictionary* (Oxford: Oxford University Press, 1971); Jaime Incer, ed., *Toponimias Indigenas de Nicaragua* (San José: Libro Libre, 1985); Miguel Asturias's novel, *Strong Wind* (New York: Dell Publishing Co., 1968) in which the word is spelled and pronounced *Amac Ric.*

(See note for part 6, "Cuzco," for further elaboration on my use of names and variant spellings.)

The epigraphs on page ix are as follows:

"Sube conmigo, amor americano." Pablo Neruda, *The Heights of Macchu Picchu*, trans. Nathaniel Tarn (New York: Farrar, Straus & Giroux, 1967), VIII, p. 39. The Tarn translation of *Heights* is an important source throughout *Hija*. Lyle Daggett's unpublished translation of *Alturas de Macchu Picchu*, and my own, were also important.

"Alberigo Vespucci . . . affects language and perceptions." Zoë Anglesey, "Central to America," an unpublished manuscript, New York, 1985. Adapted from Carew, "The Caribbean Writer and Exile."

"Contempt is the weapon . . . of a happy childhood." Alice Miller, *Prisoners of Childhood* (New York: Basic Books, 1981). [Reissued as *the Drama of the Gifted Child*, 1983.]

"The female void . . . mother-daughter body." Nor Hall, *The Moon and the Virgin: Reflections on the Archetypal Feminine* (New York: Harper & Row, 1981).

I. The Road to Quito

The Persephone-Demeter story told throughout the poem is adapted from a number of sources, mainly Thomas Bulfinch, Joseph Campbell, and the Homeric Hymn as quoted by Nor Hall, *Moon and Virgin*.

The epigraphs that open part 1 are as follows:

"Without a doubt . . . what is today Colombia." Gabriel García Márquez, "Fantasy and Artistic Creation in Latin America, The Caribbean," *Harper's Magazine*, January 1985.

"Of the time I spent in Bogotá I remember mainly images, indelible but difficult to connect." Joan Didion, *A Book of Common Prayer* (New York: Simon & Schuster, 1977).

"You will be stopped and searched many times on the road to Quito." Mary Correal, conversation with author, Bogotá, Colombia, 1979.

1. I am indebted for the motif "Out the window . . . inside the window" used throughout *Hija*, to Kenneth Koch's poem, "The Simplicity of the Unknown Past," which appeared in *The New York Review of Books*, 19 July 1979.

2. "Someone waiting for me among the violins." Neruda, *Heights*, I, p. 3.

4. "Love, love, do not come near the border." Neruda, *Heights*, VIII, p. 43.

5. "My breakaway daughter" is from the poem "Feet Like Water Lilies in Alphabet City," in "Quantum Dangers" (unpublished) by Zoë Anglesey.

The idea of "Oedipus' love of his mother" is originally from Susan Griffin, *Pornography and Silence: Culture's Revenge Against Nature* (New York: Harper & Row, 1981).

II. Quito

1a. Cerro Panecillo (Breadroll Hill) is a mountain bordering Quito. "I am the Rose ... of the valleys." Song of Solomon, *The Bible*, King James Version, 2:1.

"Everlasting rose, our home." Neruda, *Heights*, VII, p. 35.

"The collective rose" and "edifice of all mankind." Robert Pring-Mill, "Preface" to Neruda, *Heights*.

1c. The language is Quechua, the second official language of Peru and Ecuador, the language of the Incas. This is an ancient Inca chant. "There is a surging emotion in the language, which doubtlessly comes from the fact that almost all Quechua words are accented on the penultimate syllable." Von Hagen, *Realm*, p. 51.

2. "As the lily among thorns so is my love among the daughters." Solomon, 2:2. The poem "I Am the Rose of Sharon" is adapted from the entire book of the Song of Solomon, chapters 1–8.

2b. This earthquake of 23 November 1979 left fifty dead and caused widespread damage mainly in mountainous west-central Colombia.

3. "But mine own vineyard I have not kept." Solomon 1:6.

3b. Vac is the Voice that pronounced the first word, *Om*; a Hindu goddess described in the Rig Veda as the First, the Queen, the Greatest of All Deities.

3c. Omphallos (or navel) was one of the three stopping places at Eleusis. "A belly button mound of earth at the spot where Persephone disappeared. World navel where the sibyls used to sit when the voices of gods would speak through them." Hall, *Moon and Virgin*, p. 78.

3e. The Well of the Virgin is another of Demeter's resting spots. "Where the underworld and upperworld intersect. Each seat she sinks down onto in her desperation is a seething seat under which something is cooking or welling up. Consciousness has sunk so low that she is literally perched on the edge of the unconscious." Hall, *Moon and Virgin*, p. 80.

3f. "The Laughless Rock": *agelastos petra*; the third spot where Demeter stops. "Her sorrow halts nature in its path; nothing grows, life is dead. She has hardened her heart. A pallor has come over her. A dark cloak covers her shining hair. Nothing of her fruitfulness is revealed for her creativity (represented by the Maiden) has gone into hiding." Hall, *Moon and Virgin*, p. 78.

III. The Road to Lima

1b. "Who would dare to find Eurydice?" is from an unpublished, untitled poem by Michael Daley.

"Love, Love . . . Dawn on her red knees." Neruda, *Heights*, VIII, p. 39.

1c. "Baja Conmigo, Amor Americano" is derived from "Sube conmigo, amor americano." Ibid.

2. "All the sexy nuances of nada / systole and diastole." William Pitt Root, "You Ask What Poetry is These Days," *Bloomsbury Review*, September-October 1983.

3a. "When you no longer see any trees you are in Perú." "Bartolomé Ruiz, the first Spanish navigator of Perú; from his sailing instructions to Tumbes, the first port of call of the Spanish conquest." Von Hagen, *Realm*, p. 18.

"The tearlessness of arid skies that never rain." Herman Melville, *Moby Dick* (New York: Russell & Russell, Inc., 1963), p. 241.

"The end of modesty is torture, the end of pornography is murder." Griffin, *Pornography and Silence*.

IV. Lima

The epigraphs that open part 4 are as follows:

"It is the need . . . as possibility itself." Robert Creeley, "The Creative," *Sparrow 6* (Santa Barbara: Black Sparrow Press, 1973). Now in *The Collected Essays of Robert Creeley* (Berkeley and Los Angeles: University of California Press, 1989).

"Pornography is the end of lust, the final tool of capitalism." Susan Griffin, *Pornography and Silence*.

"The strangest, saddest city thou can'st see." Melville, *Moby Dick*, p. 241.

"The worst slum in the world." Carl J. Migdail, "Peru's Misery: Too Many People, Too Little Money," *U.S. News and World Report*, 11 March 1985.

2. "Buried America." Neruda, *Heights*, X, p. 58.

"We don't believe in love because we don't believe in the soul." Octavio Paz.

2a. "Deception is not / one of the Seven Sins / of your Church" is an idea from Mary Daly, *Gyn/Ecology: The Metaethics of Radical Feminism* (Boston: Beacon Press, 1979).

3. "Patriarchy the Prevailing Religion of the World." Ibid.

"Being like maize . . . like a short blade." Neruda, *Heights*, III, p. 13.

3b. "The Task of Poetry Is to Overcome Government." Brendan Behan.

3c. "We the Inca . . . to his carnal sister." Von Hagen, *Realm*, p. 125.

3f. "La Ultima Conquista de El Angel" is adapted from a book review by Bell Gale Chevigny of *La ultima conquista de El Angel,* by Elvira Orphée, which appeared in *The American Book Review* (May-June 1983) and from a review of "Tortured Women: Stories of Political Terror," by Omar Rivabella, that appeared in *Penthouse: The International Magazine for Men* (April 1985).

3g. "Everybody lost heart, anxiously waiting for death." Pablo Neruda, *The Heights of Macchu Piccho*, trans. James Wright, *James Wright: Collected Poems* (Middletown: Wesleyan University Press, 1972), III, p. 97.

4. "He who possesses rhythm possesses the universe." Charles Olson as quoted in Nor Hall, *Moon and Virgin* (New York: Harper & Row, 1980), p. 110.

5a. "Antigua América, novia sumergida." Neruda, *Heights*, X, p. 58.

5c. Yaravi (harawi). I like this interpretation the best: "There is something very ancient in this Vallejo which gives his voice a force a reader seldom confronts. It is the authority of the oral poets of the Andes, those fashioners of the 'harawi,' a mystical, inward-turning complaint. Its tones can still be heard in the homesick barrios of Lima." John Knoepfle, "Thoughts on César Vallejo," *Neruda and Vallejo: Selected Poems,* ed. Robert Bly (Boston: Beacon Press, 1971), p. 175.

6. Mamacocha is the Inca Goddess of the sea, envisioned as a great whale.

"The lips of the sea." Carlos Fuentes, *The Death of Artemus Cruz,* trans. Sam Hileman (New York: Farrar, Straus & Giroux, 1964.)

Walt Whitman is here too.

V. The Road to Cuzco

The epigraph that opens part 5 is the first paragraph of Thornton Wilder, *The Bridge of San Luis Rey* (New York: Harper & Row, 1986). The bridge, Apurimac-Chaca, was over the Apurimac River. *Apurimac* means "Great Speaker."

1. "Ecstasy Is Identity with All Existence." Peter Matthiessen, *The Snow Leopard* (New York: Viking Press, 1978), p. 42.

"Quise nadar . . . desembocaduras." Neruda, *Heights*, IV, p. 16.

"World walking." Muriel Rukeyser, "AJANTA," *Beast in View* (New York: Garden City, 1944).

"Pachamama," also, Mama Pacha. Goddess of the Crop.

"Their wounded inexistence," etc. Much of the last stanza is from Neruda, *Heights,* IV, p. 18.

2. "Queda el Alma." Neruda, *Heights,* II, p. 6.

"Mama probably cried . . . got stuck" is from "We probably already were of a compassionate age . . ." César Vallejo, *César Vallejo: The Complete Posthumous Poetry,* trans. Clayton Eshleman and José Rubia Barcia (Berkeley and Los Angeles: University of California Press, 1978), p. 19. The Spanish in the poem is from the same source.

"The famous actress wrote." Shirley MacLaine, *Out on a Limb* (New York: Bantam, 1983).

The translation from the Quechua is:
> Never fear, little brother
> little, unknown brother
> not even if you find yourself
> in a river of blood.
>
> Never fear, little brother,
> little, unknown brother,
> not even if you find yourself
> in a rain of stones.

—Barrionuevo, *Cuzco,* p. 125.

3. The opening quote is from the last paragraph of Wilder, *Bridge of San Luis Rey.*

"Oh corazón, oh frente triturada." Neruda, *Heights,* II, p. 6.

Acapana ayápcha. "*Uta* [as it is named now] is a destructive ulcerative disease [which is actually a form of leishmaniasis], which begins about the nose, and the disease eats away the nose cartilage and the lips, leaving the face horribly mutilated; it appears pictured frequently on Mochica pottery, where, incidentally, all of the native indigenous diseases are depicted. It was called, in Quechua, *acapana ayápcha,* which merely means 'red-fringed clouds,' a reference to the bleeding red walls of the face ulcer." Von Hagen, *Realm,* p. 106.

The Quechua about the *cholo* translates:
> The cholo of the radiant plain
> is like a light that brightly shines,
> all man.
> He is like an angel of ice

290

who fights with courage.

—Barrionuevo, Cuzco, p. 187.

"¡Lo entiendo ... me las pelan! ..." Vallejo, "Telúrica y magné-tica," *Complete Posthumous Poetry*, p. 88. In Eshleman's translation:

> I understand all of it on two flutes
> And I make myself understood on a quena.
> As for the others they can jerk me off.

or:

> I understand everything on two flutes
> And I make myself understood on a quena.
> Everything else leaves me cold.

"¡Auquenidos llorosos, almas mias!" Ibid.

The italicized excerpts beginning "Last Spring Edith Lagos, fifteen ... Then in March 1982 ... In September, 1982 ..." are from "Fire in the Andes," *Revolutionary Worker* 11 (February 1983).

"The CIA's policy of destabilization." John Stockwell, *In Search of Enemies: A CIA Story* (New York: Norton, 1984).

4. The Anna Livia Plurabelle quote is from James Joyce, *Work in Progress* (Winchester: Faber and Faber, 1930).

4a. The *Linga Sharira* is the ancient Hindu name for our galaxy, which we commonly call the Milky Way. The meaning of the ancient name embodies an understanding of the structure of the galaxy: *the Long Body of the Dream, the Long Body of the Tongue, the Long Body of God, the form on which the human body is molded, the Crossroads of Time and the Universe, the time when our solar system is at a right angle with the galaxy, the crossroads of the ecliptic, when the Music of the Spheres can be heard, when the Gods call for us.* The time is approximately between November 14 and 23 of each year.

4c. "The whole music breaking / full-throated into the ears," and other reverberations. Jane Hirshfield, "Lullabye," *Of Gravity & Angels* (Middletown: Wesleyan University Press, 1988).

4e. "Slick, whole body comes out of me." Sharon Olds, "The Moment the Two Worlds Meet," *The Gold Cell* (New York: Alfred A. Knopf, 1990).

5. "Psyche travels ... to be tried." Robert Duncan, "A Poem Beginning with a Line by Pindar," *The Opening of the Field* (New York: Grove Press, 1960).

5a. "And don't say another word to me / since we can kill perfectly." Vallejo, *Complete Posthumous Poetry*, Eshleman and Barcia, p. 51.

Oblomov. Title of a nineteenth-century Russian novel by Ivan Goncharov.

5b. "With your eyes . . . of starving India." Allen Ginsburg, *Kaddish and Other Poems: 1958–1960* (San Francisco: City Lights, 1961).

Coca cola. A Quechua term. *Cola* means "trader" and is the name of a tribe of Indians whose vocation is trading.

6. "Nuestro Ché: The Monroe Doctrine" is dedicated to Keith Jellum.

I am indebted to *The Death of Ché Quevarra,* by Jay Cantor; "Psychic Reading of Sharon Doubiago," by Judith Kangor; and the man named Clyde in Portland, Oregon, who insisted I use the line *"their liquid red crystals that see through the night"* in reference to the Liquid Crystal Institute Project developed at Kent State University while he was a student.

"Idiots fumbling at the bride's door. . . . I see the body of my beloved / dismembered in waking . . ." Robert Duncan, "A Poem Beginning with a Line by Pindar."

"I can't understand what being pretty has to do with the revolution." Tina Modotti, the Italian-born actress, model, photographer, communist, lover of Mexico, "pupil and partner" of Edward Weston, Diego Rivera, Frida Kahlo, etc., as quoted in a documentary film on her life that I saw in 1985 or 1986 in Portland, Oregon. See *The Day Books of Edward Weston,* ed. Nancy Newhall (New York: Aperture, 1990); Hayden Herrera, *Frida: A Biography of Frida Kahlo* (New York: Harper & Row, 1983).

VI. Cuzco

There isn't a standard spelling of the Quechua and Aymara languages. I have attempted some standardization but without a more thorough knowledge of the languages, of the Indian history and mythology, of the Spanish and English influences (and oppressions), or of the current politics, I hesitate to take liberties, even where they seem warranted. I have tended to leave the spellings as found in my sources. In obvious variants, when my emphasis has been the mythic, the historic, the indigenous, I have tried to use what seem to be the local spellings of antiquity, i.e., *Qosqo, Inka, Machupiqchu,* etc.; when the emphasis is more for simple information and description, and of the personal journey, I have used the English: *Cuzco, Inca, Macchu Picchu.* In working with the names, particularly, it is tempting to assume, for example, that *Waqaypata, the Square of Weeping,* is *Huacapata, huaca,* meaning "sacred place" or "talisman," a word I've used throughout the poem. But to change the spelling of either of these, for consistency, is dangerous. *Saikusqa,* the "tired stone" at Saqsaywaman, is possibly *saicuzca,* or *saiqosco,* since *qosco,* as in the city's full Quechua name, *Ayar Awka Qosqo Wanka,* means "marble" or "stone." Perhaps *awka* is still another variant of *huaca* (and at this point one is tempted to hear *sai* as related to our weary *sigh!*) But again, to make these assumptions would be a mistake. In English there are words with the same sounds and even spellings with entirely different meanings and etymologies. Does Quechua, like Spanish, have male/female endings, i.e., *cuzca* and *cuzco?* Other examples: *Manko/Manco. Yma Sumaq/Ima Sumac. Wayna Picchu/Piqchu/ Huana Picchu. Wayna Qhapaq/Huana Capac.* Since we spell *Quito* with the *Q,* why not *Cuzco,* especially since we know these were Inca "twin cities?" *Ecuador/Equador. Qoqa Qollo* must be *coca cola,* which must mean "coca trader," as *cola* means "trader," and is the name of a contemporary Quechua tribe. Ollanta, a historic figure, and *Tanpu,* as in *Tanpu T'oqo,* must be the source of the ruins *Ollantaytanpu/Ollantaitanpu.* Is *Asto Rimaq,* the prince that the "beautiful Inkill Chumpi of *P'isaq*" (*Pisac*) loved, related to Lima's ancient name, *Rimac?* The examples of this are endless, informative and fascinating.

Quechua "does not have the letters *b, d, f* and *j* . . . but *p, t, v* and *h* take their place. There are guttural sounds, written *cc,* which are coughed up from the bottom of the throat, as the word *ccapac* (rich). There is a double *t* at the beginning of some words which is almost impossible for one to use unless he (sic) has long spoken Quechua; thus between *tanta* (a crowd) and *ttanta* (bread) there is a vast distance in thought and pronunciation. . . . [Quechua] is so complex that one wonders how a people could verbally, without writing, transmit so expressive a tongue." Von Hagen, *Realm,* 51.

3a. "Darling Shawn." The song referred to throughout this poem is John Lennon's to his son, "beautiful boy," Sean.

"When / wilt thou redeem . . . by another undone." Luis T. Calderon Ugarte as quoted by Barrionuevo, *Cuzco,* 53.

3b. "Pacarectanpu." Barrionuevo, *Cuzco. Ayar* means "grain." Unless otherwise noted, quotations, historic facts, and mythology used throughout section 6 are from Barrionuevo, *Cuzco,* and Von Hagen, *Realm.*

3c. "In Cuzco llamas of solid gold in the Inti Pampa." Robert Duncan, "The Question," *Opening of the Field.*

"Outside eleven thousand llamas." Márquez, *Harper's Magazine,* January 1985.

4. "Stick step . . . from another stick." Vallejo, "GLEBE," *Complete Posthumous Poetry,* Eshleman and Barcia.

5. "The pucara . . . reared by man." Von Hagen, *Realm,* p. 161.

"If coca did not exist—neither would Peru." Pedro de Cieza de León as quoted by Von Hagen, *Realm*, p. 110.

"Some historians think . . . razor between them." Barrionuevo, *Cuzco*, p. 147.

6. "Viraqocha, Lord of the Universe . . . can work magic" is an ancient Peruvian prayer preserved on the quipu.

8. "We Peruvians . . . and loneliness companionable." Barrionuevo, *Cuzco*, p. 9.

Tupaq Amaru: the last Inca ruler. Tupaq Amaru II: the Indians rose in rebellion in 1780 under his leadership.

9. "Porque mi patria es hermosa." Juan Louis Dammert, *Porque mi patria es hermosa* (Lima: Ediciones Aquardienre, 1976).

VII. The Heights of Macchu Picchu

The epigraphs that open part 7 are from the following:

"The Homeric Hymn . . . spiritual survival." Adrienne Rich, *Of Woman Born: Motherhood as Experience and Institution* (New York: Norton, 1986), p. 240.

"Eleusis . . . called the Kore." Hall, *Moon and Virgin*, p. 75.

"There, in the great blaze of light . . . sever them entirely." Rich, *Of Woman Born*, p. 241.

The Spanish throughout this section is from Neruda's *Alturas de Macchu Picchu*; there are also references, allusions, and direct translations to English by Nathaniel Tarn and myself.

2. "Then up the ladder . . . Macchu Picchu." Neruda, *Heights*, VI.

2b. "Stone within stone . . . where was he." Neruda, *Heights*, X, p. 57.

4a. I am indebted to Pat Monaghan's manuscript, "Sun Goddess," in which she traces the sun as female through many cultures.

5. "As the daughter is the core of the mother." Judith Roche, "Memory Is the Future," *Poetry Flash* (July 1986).

"Positive / sun ions. Negative / thundering falls ions." Susu Jeffrey, in a letter to the author.

Manko and Raymi were the first Inca gods.

"Central to America" is from Anglesey, "Central to America."

6a. "Now to tread the dance / Now to tread the light" is from Aristophanes' *Lysistrata*, trans. Donald Sutherland (New York: Harper & Row, 1961).

6c. The first two stanzas are paraphrases of Dinnerstein, *Mermaid and Minotaur*.

"The coffin of gender." Louise Glück, "On Stanley Kunitz," *American Poetry Review*, 14, no. 5 (September-October 1985).

8. "Up here men's feet ... come death." *Heights,* Tarn, VI, p. 29.

9. "Your eyes / of ancient / glacier water." Carolyn Kizer, "Antigue Father," *Yin* (Brockport: Boa Editions, 1984), p. 62.

10a. Midnight, November 3–4, 1979, Macchu Picchu, Peru

First House:	8° 57' Leo. Mars 22° 28' Leo; Jupiter 6° 11' Virgo; North Node 6° 23' Virgo Retrograde.
Second House:	13° 32' Virgo. Saturn 23° 36' Virgo.
Third House:	17° 49' Libra, Pluto 20° 00 Libra; Sun 11° 11' Scorpio.
Fourth House:	18° 20' Scorpio; Uranus 20° 40' Scorpio; Venus 29° 39' Scorpio; Mercury 3° 59' Sagittarius. A fixed star is here also.
Fifth House:	15° 13' Sagittarius; Neptune 18° 50' Sagittarius.
Sixth House:	11° 00 Capricorn. Part of Fortune 8° 31' Aquarius
Seventh House:	8° 57' Aquarius. South Node 6° 23' Pisces.
Eighth House:	13° 32' Pisces.
Ninth House:	17° 49' Aries. Moon 10° 44' Taurus.
Tenth House:	18° 20' Taurus.
Eleventh House:	15° 13' Gemini.
Twelfth House:	11° 00 Cancer.

—Carol McMaines, Astrologer, Portland, Oregon.

(For an explanation of the *Linga Sharira* see note for part 5, "The Road to Cuzco," 4a.)

10b. "I have a small daughter." Mary Barnard, trans., *Sappho: A New Translation* (Berkeley and Los Angeles: University of California Press, 1958).

Epilogue: The Dawn, Amor Amerrique

Amor Amerrique is derived from Neruda, "Amor América (1400)," trans. Lyle Daggett, *DALMO'MA* 7 (Port Townsend, Empty Bowl, 1986), pp. 1–2.

The epigraphs that open the epilogue are from the following:

"From my mother's sleep ... turret with a hose." Randall Jarrell, "Death of the Ball Turret Gunner," *The Complete Poems* (New York: Farrar, Straus & Giroux, 1969).

"Mother ... tiniest star." Jack Hirschman, "Mother," *The Bottom Line* (Connecticut: Curbstone Press, 1988).

"What is this mother-father ... new Eve who comes." H. D., "Tribute to the Angels," *Trilogy* (New York: New Directions, 1973).

"I come to speak through your dead mouths." Neruda, *Heights*, XII, p. 68.

"What would happen ... would split open." Muriel Rukeyser, "Kathë Kollwitz," *No More Masks*, eds. Bass & Howe (New York: Doubleday-Anchor Books, 1973), p. 103.

"But the longer ... in godhead." Robert Graves, *The White Goddess* (New York: Farrar, Straus & Giroux, 1948), p. 486.

Again, I am—*we are*—profoundly indebted to Dorothy Dinnerstein. And also to Robert Graves, H. D., and the many works of anthropology on the Goddess religion of the ancient world.

2. "I, Incan ... and I said." Neruda, "Amor América (1400)."

3. "Her body is a vessel of death / Devouring hole. Abyss." Susan Griffin, *Of Women and Nature: The Roaring Inside Her* (New York: Harper & Row, 1979), p. 183.

4. "The male-female collaboration to keep history mad has become impossible to sustain." Dinnerstein, *Mermaid and Minotaur.*

4a. "Who comes to recognize himself as 'Other.' " Ibid.

Acknowledgments

I would like to extend my gratitude here to the following people who either aided us in our journey or aided me in the writing of it: Efrain Correal who sent us to his mother, Mary Correal, and sister Patricia, in Bogotá, Colombia; Quen Clark who as a single woman made the journey before us and encouraged us to make it also; Devreaux Baker who gave me her abalone necklace to ward off sorrow, to bring good luck; Juan Louis Dammert and Marisol Ballo, poets of Miraflores, Peru; Bruce Black for his *Letter of Introduction* from Chief Peacock of Orem, Utah (saved us in Huancayo); Pat Fitzgerald, Finn Wilcox, Dane and Shi Shi Fitzgerald for a decade of important, supportive friendship; Maryna Albert who caught my "classic" mistake (originally the poem was addressed to the lover rather than to the daughter); Judith Roche for the years of friendship, the continuing conversation that has made me aware of the importance of the Mother/Son paradigm of ancient history; Carolyn Forché for great generosity of friendship and poetic Pan-American inspiration; Beth Bosk and *The New Settler Interview* for continuing support of my ecofeminist work; Lyle Daggett who helped me to find Dorothy Dinnerstein; Carolyn Kizer, Judith Tannenbaum, Meridel Le Sueur, Jack Hirschman, and Sarah Menefee who read and critiqued the original manuscript; the U-Cross Foundation, the Montalvo Association, the Wolfpen Writers' Colony, and the Djerassi Foundation for residencies; and/or Arts Grant, Seattle, Washington, 1984 ($700 for an "experimental poem" about a mother-daughter journey to South America); my towns, especially Mendocino, Ashland, and Port Townsend—*mi huacas;* the young women at Rosemont School, Portland, Oregon, who were there at the end. Epic thanks and gratitude, too, to my publisher and editors, Ed Ochester and Beth Detwiler. And to all my family, nuclear and extended, who have given me love, vision, poetry, and strength—most especially my exemplary, extraordinary mother, Audrey Garnet Clarke Edens.

About the Author

SHARON LURA EDENS DOUBIAGO was born in Long Beach, California. She holds an M.A. degree in English from California State University, Los Angeles, and for many years has traveled the American West as an itinerant writer and artist-in-residence at numerous schools and colleges. She received the 1991 Hazel Hall Oregon Book Award for Poetry for *Psyche Drives the Coast, Poems 1974–1987*. She considers the West Coast of the United States—San Diego to Seattle, Ramona to Port Townsend—her home.

Pitt Poetry Series

Ed Ochester, General Editor